CULTURES OF THE WORLD

ISRAEL

Jill DuBois

MARSHALL CAVENDISH
New York • London • Sydney

Reference Edition published 1999 by
Marshall Cavendish Corporation
99 White Plains Road
Tarrytown
New York 10591

© Times Editions Pte Ltd 1995, 1993

Originated and designed by
Times Books International, an imprint of
Times Editions Pte Ltd

Printed in Singapore

Library of Congress Cataloging-in-Publication Data:
DuBois, Jill, 1952–
    Israel / Jill DuBois.
      p. cm.—(Cultures Of The World)
    Includes bibliographical references and index.
    Summary: Discusses the geography, history, government,
economy, and culture of the country that is a Holy Land for
Jews, Christians, and Muslims.
    ISBN 1-85435-531-7 (vol.):   —ISBN 1-85435-529-5 (set)
    1. Israel—Juvenile literature. [1. Israel.]
I. Title. II. Series.
DS102.95.D82 1992
956.94—dc20   92–10208
                    CIP
                  AC

INTRODUCTION

ISRAEL IS A SMALL, YOUNG NATION in a land with a lengthy, rich past that spans the ages. Its ancient history can be read in the Bible, yet as a modern state it is less than a half century old.

Transformed from a vast desert and swamp wasteland into thriving farmlands and flourishing orchards in a few short decades, it is the pride of the Jews. Israel is the holy land for three of the world's great religions, and though it is a Jewish state, Christians, Muslims, and Jews live there in relative harmony. Nonetheless, the fragile peace can be and has been broken. As part of the series *Cultures of the World*, this book will familiarize you with the attitudes, beliefs, and lifestyles of the passionate people living in one of the most controversial countries in the world.

CONTENTS

A Palestine sunbird drinking water.

CONTENTS

The Jerusalem Theater.

GEOGRAPHY

THE REPUBLIC OF ISRAEL is an ancient land which has been in existence as a national state for the Jewish people for less than 50 years.

Occupying most of what was formerly Palestine, Israel is located in the Middle East, on the eastern shore of the Mediterranean Sea. Geographically, it belongs to the Asian continent, but it acts as a bridge connecting Asia, Africa, and Europe. It is bounded to the north by Lebanon, to the northeast by Syria, and its southernmost tip extends to the Gulf of Aqaba and the Red Sea. To the east and southeast is Jordan, and to the southwest is Egypt.

Israel has a total area of about 8,020 square miles, making it approximately the size of the state of Massachusetts. It is a long slice of land, with its width as narrow as 10 miles in some areas and no wider than 70 miles at any point.

Its present borders include the following: the Israel-Lebanon Armistice Line; the Israel-Syria Disengagement Line after the Yom Kippur War; the Israel-Jordan Ceasefire Line after the Six Day War, and the Israel-Egypt boundary according to a peace treaty in 1979.

Above: **The Mushroom Rock in the Avara Valley.**

Opposite: **Flowers in full bloom on a hillside in Israel during spring.**

Despite its small size, Israel contains almost every type of geographical terrain: mountains, subtropical valleys, deserts, and fertile land with a rich variety of plants and animals.

Israel is the first Jewish state to be established in nearly 2,000 years. Its creation represents a prophecy fulfilled from the Bible where God promised the land to the Jewish people. This was also the desire of the Jews, who wanted a nation that did not need to depend on others for help.

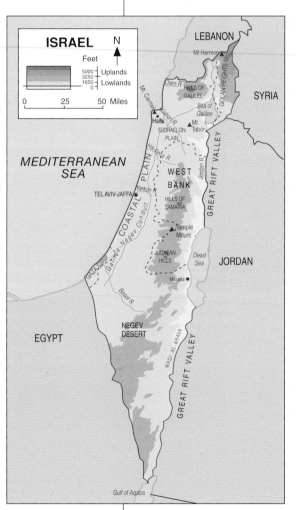

ISRAEL N

Feet

5000
3250 Uplands
1650 Lowlands
0

0   25   50 Miles

LEBANON

Mt Hermon

MEDITERRANEAN
SEA

SYRIA

HILLS OF
GALILEE

Sea of
Galilee

GOLAN HEIGHTS

Haifa

ESDRAELON
PLAIN

Mt.
Tabor

GREAT RIFT VALLEY

TEL AVIV-JAFFA

WEST
BANK

HILLS OF
SAMARIA

Jordan R.

GAZA STRIP

COASTAL PLAIN

Galilee-Negev Conduit

Temple
Mount

JUDAEAN
HILLS

Dead
Sea

JORDAN

Masada

Besor R.

EGYPT

NEGEV
DESERT

WADI AL-ARAVA

GREAT RIFT VALLEY

Gulf of Aqaba

TOPOGRAPHY

Four geographical features are prominent: hills in the northern and central regions, the western coastal plain, the Jordan rift or Great Rift Valley in the east, and the Negev Desert in the south.

There are three distinct hilly regions. The hills of Galilee to the north has the highest mountain in Israel, Mount Meron (3,926 feet). This range has much rainfall and fertile valleys that produce tobacco and olives. South of the hills of Galilee is the hot, humid but fertile Esdraelon Plain, formerly a swampland. Upland plateaus lie south of the plain.

The western coastal plain and most populated region includes Tel Aviv and the principal port Haifa. This heartland of Israel has citrus plantations, planned settlements, and industries.

The Great Rift Valley is a deep depression formed millions of years ago when the floor of the Jordan River valley and the Dead Sea collapsed. It extends south approximately 274 miles and is dominated by the Jordan River, the Sea of Galilee, and the Dead Sea.

The Negev Desert comprises more than half of Israel's total land area. It was once almost 20% larger than it is now, but agricultural development has decreased its size. Located here are many kibbutzim ("key-BOOT-zim") and moshavim ("MOH-shau-vim"), the agricultural settlements of Israel.

SEAS AND RIVERS

The most important river in Israel is the Jordan. It originates in the Golan Heights in the north, runs southward near the borders of Lebanon and Syria, through the Sea of Galilee, and empties into the Dead Sea.

The Yarkon and the Kishon rivers are the only other waterways with permanent flows; others are dry throughout most of the year. The Yarkon runs into the Mediterranean near Tel Aviv, and the Kishon does so near Haifa. Both the Jordan and the Yarkon are irrigation sources for the Negev Desert.

The National Water Carrier, a freshwater pipeline system from the Sea of Galilee, provides drinking as well as irrigation water to the desert. Also known as Lake Kinneret or Tiberias, the Sea of Galilee is a very popular vacation and fishing area.

The Dead Sea is a large saltwater lake that is almost three times as salty as the Mediterranean. It is 1,300 feet below sea level, making it the lowest place on earth. Its salt content is so high that the land around it cannot be cultivated, but its water is said to have certain healing qualities.

Pillars of salt in the mysterious Dead Sea.

The Dead Sea has such a high mineral content that even a non-swimmer can float on its surface! It cannot sustain fish or plant life, thereby deserving its name. However, it has great commercial value as it is one of the world's largest sources of potash, as well as a plentiful source of magnesium bromide, magnesium chloride, and salt. It is also the site of the biblical cities of Sodom and Gomorrah, which were completely destroyed.

CLIMATE

The climate of Israel has been characterized as Mediterranean, which means that it has two seasons: winter—which lasts from November to March—and summer—which lasts from April to October.

During the summer there is little rain, and temperatures reach around the high 80s even on the coast. Summer temperatures are warmer in the desert, mountain ranges, and valleys. Nearly 70% of the annual rainfall takes place during the winter.

Because of Israel's location between desert and the humid Mediterranean Sea, rainfall is not evenly distributed throughout the country. In the south, the average rainfall is one-tenth that of the north. Temperatures differ from north to south as well. In the summer, cool breezes prevail in Jerusalem, while the desert can be as hot as 120°F.

One particularly bothersome part of Israel's weather is its windstorms. Hot desert winds that carry dust and sand can lower humidity and raise temperatures to almost unbearable levels.

FLORA AND FAUNA

There is plenty of plant life in Israel, from blooming plants to brushes and shrubs. It is believed that more than 2,000 species grow here, with wild flowers dotting the mountains and valleys, and cacti adorning the desert. In fact, the native Israeli is known as a sabra, or "prickly pear," named after the cactus fruit, which is tough on the outside but sweet on the inside.

Flowers are so plentiful here that the country began selling cut flowers in the 1960s and, in 20 years, Israel grew into Europe's largest supplier. Tulips, roses, anemones, irises, poppies, and cyclamen are among the many blooms found in Israel.

For centuries trees covered Israel's mountains, but lumber and firewood needs, years of cultivation, and food for goats and sheep, combined with erosion from the sometimes violent, cyclone-like desert storms, destroyed much vegetation.

However, there has been a successful and aggressive reforestation program underway for many decades. Millions of trees have been planted under the program. Species of trees and brush that do survive are Aleppo pines, and Tabor and evergreen oaks. Almond and fruit trees, such as olive, date, and fig, are also abundant.

There are several wildlife reserves in Israel, which are mainly inhabited by water birds and smaller animals. These include parts of the region of Arava in the south, Mount Carmel, Mount Meron, and the Hula Lake and marshes in the north. Pelicans, herons, partridges, and varieties of desert and mountain birds are some of the estimated 360 species found there.

Animals such as wildcats, gazelles, mongooses, jackals, foxes, weasels, wild boars, hares, badgers, and hyenas live in the Jordan River valley and near the Dead Sea. Snakes and lizards are found in the Negev Desert and other areas with desert-like conditions.

CITIES

The largest cities in Israel are Jerusalem (with 504,100 people), Tel Aviv-Jaffa (328,000), and Haifa (235,000). Approximately 85% of Israel's inhabitants live in towns and cities. Smaller Israeli cities include Beersheba (with 110,000), Netanya (102,000), Elat (19,000), and others like Hebron, Rehovot, Ashdod, and Shechem.

JERUSALEM

Jerusalem is the capital of the Jewish state (though it is not recognized as such by the United Nations; most foreign governments maintain their embassies in Tel Aviv). Like many cities whose past spans the ages, it is an exciting mixture of old and new.

One very interesting feature of this ancient city is that it is a holy city for three distinct religions. In addition to its importance for the Jews, it holds great significance for Christians and Muslims. It is the historical, spiritual, and national center of the Jewish people since King David proclaimed it the capital of the land in 1000 B.C. For Christians, it is the site of Jesus' crucifixion, burial, and resurrection. For Muslims, it is their third holy city.

For much of modern history, Jerusalem has been divided into two parts, the Jordanian and Israeli sectors. After 1967, the whole city came under Israel's control. Today, there is the Old City and the New City.

THE OLD CITY The Old City, which is in the eastern part of Jerusalem, is territory taken from Jordan during the Six Day War in 1967. It has since been integrated with the newer sections of the city. The New City is west of the Old City and has wider streets and modern buildings.

The Old City section is easily identified because it remains enclosed

Until 1860, Jerusalem was a walled city made up of four distinct quarters: Jewish, Muslim, Armenian, and Christian. After 1860, a growing Jewish population began to establish new neighborhoods outside the walls. Since then, Jews have become the majority community in the city.

within the walls built by the Ottoman Empire's Suleiman the Magnificent in the 16th century.

There are five sections within the Old City: the revived Jewish Quarter, with its fragmented historical remains, was destroyed and rebuilt many times; the Christian Quarter, with its Holy Sepulchre; the Armenian Quarter, a residential area with ancient buildings, churches, and chapels; the densely populated Muslim Quarter, containing the ancient temple area; and the Temple Mount, location of the Western (Wailing) Wall and the eight-sided Dome of the Rock, where the prophet Mohammed is believed to have ascended to heaven.

The Temple Mount, because of its importance to Jews and Muslims alike, remains one of Jerusalem's most troublesome spots. The Old City has been declared "a protected cultural monument" by UNESCO.

Another area of great controversy is the city's West Bank, where more than 700,000 Palestinians live. This area is on the western side of the Jordan River, and because it has not been made a part of Israel, the Palestinians living here do not have the political rights that Arabs in other parts of Israel have. They are free to take jobs in Israel, but their wages are often quite low. They are not governed by Israeli law, and are often subject to mass arrests and occasional mistreatment.

Thousands of Jews have moved into the West Bank since the establishment of the occupied areas because of the low-cost housing available there. This has angered the Arabs and, as a result, the West Bank remains a spot of frequent unrest.

The Ecce Homo Arch over part of the Via Dolorosa in Jerusalem. The arch is believed to be where Pontius Pilate showed Jesus Christ to the crowd before the crucifixion.

Jerusalem at night.

THE NEW CITY The New City itself is not as spectacular as the Old City, and the name is misleading because parts of it are quite old. It has many areas that have great religious significance, such as the Garden of Gethsemane where Jesus prayed before he was arrested and crucified, the Mount of Olives and its ancient Jewish cemetery, and Mount Zion and King David's tomb. It also has office towers, high-rises, wide streets, and lovely parks.

It is the capital of the Jewish state because of its importance to Judaism. It is the seat of the parliament or Knesset ("kuh-NESS-et"), and home to the Hebrew University. The National Museum as well as important government and commercial institutions are also located here. The core of the city is commercial and residential, and its limited industrial areas are on the outskirts.

Jerusalem has two very distinct features. All of its older buildings are made of Jerusalem stone, which gives the city a uniform look. Also, it has a special fragrance, known as "Jerusalem Perfume," that is actually the scent of wild flowers that wafts through the air in the evening. This lovely aroma disappears when it is burned off with the morning sun.

TEL AVIV-JAFFA

Tel Aviv, which means "hill of spring," is a city that is over 80 years old. It was founded by a group of European immigrants who had been living in the Arab town of Jaffa, a neighboring seaport. This town grew rapidly within a short time and is characteristic of the fast pace that still exists there today. Tel Aviv united with Jaffa to become one city some 40 years ago. Because of the melding of two cities, the Tel Aviv-Jaffa area is also an interesting combination of old and new.

Tel Aviv, with Dizengof Square in the center.

Tel Aviv is a bustling city and the industrial center of Israel. It is home to many foreign embassies because, although Israel declared Jerusalem its capital, many countries do not recognize it as Israeli territory. Tel Aviv is the entertainment and art center of Israel, boasting numerous theater groups and museums, and there are beautiful white beaches that hug the blue waters of the Mediterranean Sea. As a modern metropolis, however, it also suffers the problems of other big cities, including traffic jams, urban poverty, and development problems.

Jaffa, on the other hand, is the legendary port from which the prophet Jonah set sail before being consumed by a great fish. In Jaffa today, there are open markets and old forts that were built hundreds of years before the birth of Jesus Christ.

This city retains its Eastern character, perhaps because thousands of Israel's North African and Asian Jews reside here. The narrow alleys and streets are home to many artists, and among their stalls are outdoor cafés and beautiful antique shops. The port, said to be one of the oldest in the world, served as an entry point to thousands of Jews who came to start a new life. Its harbor is now closed to commercial shipping.

HAIFA

Haifa was built on the slopes of Mount Carmel in the early 1900s, due in large part to the establishment of the Haifa-Damascus Railway. In 1929, the British built a modern harbor there and Haifa became an important shipping center. It remains Israel's major Mediterranean port.

Israel's heavy industrial center is also in the Haifa area. Petroleum refineries, automobile and tire manufacturers, glass factories, cement works, steel mills, fertilizer producers, and shipbuilders are all located here.

Despite its prosperous industrial focus, Haifa is a splendid city whose beauty has been compared to that of San Francisco. It is also the world center for the Baha'i faith.

Haifa with the beautiful Mediterranean Sea in the background.

THE OCCUPIED TERRITORIES

After the 1967 Six Day War, more than a million Palestinian Arabs from the Gaza Strip, East Jerusalem and the West Bank, and the Golan Heights came under Israeli rule. These Arabs were ruled by a military administration, and none of them are Israeli citizens.

Because of the *Intifada*, an ongoing uprising that began in the West Bank and the Gaza Strip and continues today in other Arab communities, these Palestinians were at times subjected to mass arrests. The Israelis cited security considerations to justify these acts.

Palestinians in the occupied territories were allowed to hold local elections and establish laws through their own legal system, and visit with their relatives in Jordan through an "open bridge" policy. Health care, education, housing, and other services were available to the residents of the territories.

The occupied territories are the following areas:

WEST BANK: This area is bounded by Israel on three sides and by the Dead Sea and the Jordan River to the east. It covers 2,270 square miles and has a population of 923,000—75% of whom are Arabs. It includes what was formerly the Jordanian section of Jerusalem. In 1988, King Hussein of Jordan gave up claims to the West Bank so that the Palestinians there could establish an independent state.

GOLAN HEIGHTS: Located at the point where Israel meets Syria to the southeast of Lebanon, it is a mountainous region of approximately 600 square miles. Though occupied by Israel during the 1967 war, the area was formally placed under Israeli "law, jurisdiction, and administration" in 1981. This territory is mainly occupied by Druze Arabs. The population of the Golan Heights is approximately 25,500.

GAZA STRIP: This is the part of Palestine that is adjacent to the Sinai Desert. Gaza was held by Egypt after the ceasefire in the War of Independence, and since then was not legally a part of any country. The territory has approximately 614,000 people living in refugee camps, nearly double the number just 20 years ago.

Beginning May 13, 1994, Israel handed over the Gaza Strip and the West Bank town of Jericho to the Palestinians to govern. Talks are expected to follow on limited Palestinian self-rule in the rest of the West Bank and a withdrawal of Israeli troops from the Golan Heights, although these events are not expected to take place soon.

HISTORY

THE HISTORY OF THE LAND OF ISRAEL is closely related to the growth of the Jewish people. It is a blending of national and religious traditions dating back thousands of years to the era of the biblical patriarchs Abraham, Isaac, and Jacob. The Bible serves as Israel's principal historical source for its ancient period, perhaps the most famous and talked about of all ancient civilizations.

Yet modern Israel is not even a half century old. Because of its prime location at the crossroads of Europe, Africa, and Asia, Israel was always the target of conquerors. And its great importance to three of the world's great religions—Christianity, Islam, and Judaism—has intensified the conflicts that characterize its great but troubled history.

Opposite: **Parts of the Old City in Jerusalem, with the Citadel and Tower of David in the background.**

Left: **Crusader forts in the ruins of Caesarea, an ancient port on the Mediterranean coast.**

Ruins at Tel Hazor, the important biblical city that King Solomon used to control the northern borders of his kingdom.

EARLY HISTORY

Israel's history begins around 1800 B.C. with the migration of a group of nomads, led by Abraham, eastward from Mesopotamia. Setting up tents and digging wells, the nomads settled in Canaan ("KAY-nan," Palestine's former name) and called the settlement Beersheba. Known as the Ivrim ("IH-vhrim," Hebrews), they wandered around Canaan for about three generations, until a famine forced them to migrate once again.

Abraham's grandson, Jacob (also known as Israel), relocated with his 12 sons and their families to Egypt. These families grew in numbers, eventually became 12 tribes, and were collectively known as Israelites. They remained in the Nile River delta region for several centuries, and the Egyptian pharaohs eventually enslaved them.

Around 1300 B.C., the prophet Moses led the Israelites out of Egypt and slavery. Under his guidance, they wandered around the Sinai Peninsula between Palestine and Egypt. During that time, Moses convinced the people that there is only one God—whom the Israelites called Yahweh ("yah-WEY"). The Israelites made a covenant, or sacred agreement, to worship only God and follow His laws, the Ten Commandments. The Commandments gave purpose and unity to the different tribes.

Around 1250 B.C., the 12 tribes returned to Canaan under the guidance of Joshua, who succeeded Moses. They encountered the Philistines, who had recently been forced from their homeland of Crete, and the Canaanites, who did not want the Israelites to settle there. For the next 200 years, these three groups fought for Canaan.

The Canaanites proved to be the weakest group; by around 1125 B.C., the Israelites had defeated them. However, the Philistines (after whom Palestine was named) had a superior military organization and better weapons. About 1050 B.C., they defeated the Israelites, causing the 12 tribes to unite for strength under one king. Under Saul, however, there was dissension that continued until his death. David succeeded Saul and was able to unite the armies to defeat the Philistines and take over Canaan.

The remains of the main gate and city walls of biblical Shechem.

David established Jerusalem as the capital of the kingdom of Israel and began building the city. Upon his death, his son Solomon became king and completed the city and its magnificent stone temple in which the Israelites could worship God. However, after Solomon's death, the different tribes began feuding and they split the kingdom into two parts—Israel, with its capital at Samaria in the north, was home to 10 tribes, and Judah, with its capital at Jerusalem in the south, was home to the remaining two tribes. Citizens of the southern portion became known as Jews.

Over the next few centuries, the two Hebrew kingdoms engaged in occasional fighting while trying to fend off attacks from outsiders.

An Israeli archer during the time of the war with the Assyrian empire in the 8th century B.C.

UNDER FOREIGN RULE

In the early 8th century B.C., the Assyrians from the north attacked and conquered Israel, exiling some and taking others as slaves. Legend has it that those who were exiled, known as the Ten Lost Tribes, never returned to the Holy Land. Nearly 200 years later, the Chaldeans under Nebuchadnezzar came and conquered Judah and destroyed the temple in Jerusalem. The remaining Jews were exiled to the Babylonian empire.

The Hebrews were freed less than 50 years later when Cyrus the Great of Persia conquered the Babylonians. Cyrus allowed the Jews to return to their homeland and rebuild the temple. However, Palestine remained under the control of the Persians for another two centuries.

In 331 B.C., the Persian empire collapsed after being attacked by Alexander the Great of Macedonia. Alexander allowed self government and religious freedom for the Jews because he respected their monotheism (belief in one God). Later, the Ptolemies ("TAHL-eh-miz") of Egypt and the Seleucids ("seh-LOO-sidz") of Syria succeeded Alexander for control of the region. Eventually, the Macedonians tried to impose their religion on the Jews. But under the guidance of a warrior named Judas Maccabee, the Jews revolted. Although Judas died, the Jews re-established their independence in 141 B.C. after prolonged fighting.

Less than a century later, however, the Jewish state was occupied once again, this time by the Romans. The land became a part of the Roman empire in 63 B.C., when it was renamed Judea. Over the next century, the Jews clashed with the Roman rulers, for they wanted to maintain their own religion and independence. Spurred on by a group known as the Zealots, the Jews launched the Great Revolt against the Romans. In the process, the Romans destroyed Jerusalem and its temple in A.D. 70, leaving all but the Western Wall in ruins.

MASADA

The strong will of the Jewish people to retain their freedom and their land goes back to ancient times. In A.D. 70, after Jerusalem fell to the Romans, freedom fighters known as the Zealots took refuge in a fortress high up a mountain known as Masada. A Roman army of 15,000 came to fight this Jewish force of less than 1,000. But it took them almost two years and a battering ram to eventually break through Masada's protective wall.

Realizing that they were outnumbered and that, at the very best, a life of slavery was all that was in store for them, the Zealots committed suicide rather than be captured. Under the leadership of Eleazar Ben Jair, the remaining 960 Jews organized and executed a mass suicide to ensure a hollow Roman victory.

Masada underwent extensive archeological digs in the 1960s, though it was identified more than a century before by two American scientists. Bones unearthed at the site have undergone radiocarbon dating tests, which determined that the skeletons are probably those of the Jewish rebels who killed themselves rather than surrender to the Romans.

One last revolt against the Romans took place in A.D. 132: Simon Bar-Kochba led Jewish fighters against the Roman empire for about three years before being crushed. To ensure that the Jews would not rise again, the Roman Emperor Hadrian destroyed Jerusalem and prohibited the Jews from setting foot in it. He renamed the area Palestine to remind the Jews of their early foes, the Philistines.

The Romans then deported the Jews to colonies throughout the known world. This scattering, known as the Diaspora ("die-uh-SPORE-uh"), sent most of the Jews to the shores of the Black Sea, the Greek Islands, and the coasts of the Mediterranean Sea. Some Jews fled to northern Europe and areas eastward. Regardless of where they settled, the Jews clung to their religious and cultural roots, one day hoping to return to their land.

Below: **Crusaders storm the walls of Jerusalem during the Crusades.**

THE FIGHT FOR PALESTINE

Palestine remained under Roman rule for the next 500 years. During that time, Christianity gained importance, as followers of Jesus of Nazareth spread his gospel.

Later, the Byzantine empire took over Roman rule after the fall of Rome in A.D. 476. These rulers did not take the rise of Islam seriously and underestimated the Arab military. The Arabs attacked and, after two years, conquered Jerusalem. For the next 460 years, the country remained under Muslim rule. Some exiled Jews returned to Palestine during this time.

The early years of Arab rule were acceptable to the Jews, but later, the Muslim spiritual rulers introduced restrictions on non-Muslims, including heavy land taxes. At this time, because of Jerusalem's importance to Christianity, soldiers from Europe launched a crusade to take the land back from Muslim rule. The Crusaders conquered Jerusalem and most of Palestine, and ruled for the next two centuries.

In 1187, a Muslim

army under Saladin recaptured Jerusalem. After Saladin's death, the Christians regained it, but only until 1291, when the Egyptian Mamluks took it, returning Muslim rule to Palestine for the next two and a half centuries. During this time, increasing number of Jews returned to the Holy Land. By 1517, the Mamluks had been overthrown by the Ottomans. The Ottomans removed all Mamluk administrators, divided Palestine into districts, and allowed the Jewish community to expand.

Jewish colonies grew and Jews from France, Germany, Portugal, Spain, and the Orient migrated to Palestine. The dream of re-establishing a homeland began to take shape.

Tourists at a Crusader fortress in the ruins of Caesarea by the Mediterranean Sea.

Chaim Weizmann, the first president of Israel, meeting British Foreign Secretary Arthur Balfour (standing).

ESTABLISHING A HOMELAND

Several historical events helped establish the Israeli homeland. The idea of creating a Jewish state became known as the Zionist movement. In 1878, Jews purchased farmland in Palestine to set up a community. The first modern Jewish village was thus established. Around that time, there was much oppression of, and violence against, Jews in Eastern Europe. Four years later, an organized group of Jews fleeing Europe emigrated to Palestine. This immigration is called the First Aliyah ("ah-lee-YUH").

Zionism began in 1897 when Theodor Herzl created the World Zionist Organization, one year after writing *The Jewish State*, a leaflet in which he suggested that Jews emigrate to Palestine from countries where they were persecuted. Herzl's efforts inspired the Second Aliyah in 1904. Waves of immigrants entered Palestine after that and created agricultural settlements throughout the country.

During World War I, British Foreign Secretary Arthur Balfour declared that his government favored "the establishment in Palestine of a national home for the Jewish people." Shortly thereafter, British forces defeated the Ottoman Empire and captured Palestine.

By this time, the Arabs also wanted independence. They saw the fall of the Ottoman empire as the opportunity for them to claim Palestine as their own, regardless of what the British government proposed. Despite the promise that the civil and religious rights of Arabs and Jews would be safeguarded, the roots of conflict were established. The British would rule over Palestine until 1948.

Between 1919 and 1933, the number of Jews in Palestine more than tripled to 200,000. As more Jewish oppression and persecution took place

in Europe, Arab aggression against Palestinian Jews also increased and they revolted against British control. By 1937, the British realized that dividing the land was the best solution, but they limited the number of Jews that could emigrate to Israel and proposed the start of Arab and Jewish states within 10 years.

The crimes against Jews in World War II—six million European Jews were killed by the Nazis in the Holocaust—produced worldwide sympathy and support for the Zionist movement. Though the immigration limit remained in effect, some European Jews with nowhere to go managed to enter Palestine. By 1946, the Jewish community grew to nearly 700,000.

After the war, the question of Palestine came up again. Since they could satisfy neither side, Britain placed the issue of dividing the land with the United Nations before leaving the region. The United Nations recommended that Palestine be divided into separate Arab and Jewish states, with Jerusalem having special international status. The Arabs rejected the plan. On May 14, 1948, Israel declared itself an independent state.

THE WAR YEARS

Within 24 hours of the British leaving the land, the combined forces of Lebanon, Jordan, Egypt, and Iraq attacked. The Israeli defense troops fought with weapons and the few planes left behind by the British, and with the help of generous donations from nations and individuals. After several months of fighting, a peace treaty was signed in January 1949. Israel had gained 50% more land than it had been given, as well as half of Jerusalem. The Arab nations, meanwhile, imposed an economic boycott on Israel.

The first Israeli elections were held after the ceasefire, with Chaim Weizmann elected president and David Ben-Gurion prime minister. The new government was admitted into the United Nations in May 1949.

Clashes with Syria at the border started in the 1960s. When Israel

Israeli tanks approaching the Golan Heights during the Yom Kippur War.

An Israeli soldier carrying a wounded comrade to safety during the period of heaviest fighting at the Golan Heights.

threatened to fight back, Syria enlisted the help of Egypt. On June 5, 1967, Israel simultaneously attacked Egypt, Syria, and Jordan. It took only six days for the Israeli army to totally defeat its enemies. After the ceasefire, Israel had increased its land size by nearly 200%, conquering the Golan Heights, the Sinai Peninsula, and the West Bank of the Jordan River, plus all of Jerusalem. Meanwhile, the Palestine Liberation Organization (PLO), a force of guerrilla fighters, stepped up its attacks on Israel and Jews throughout the world. These attacks included hijacking airplanes and killing Israeli athletes at the 1972 Olympics in Germany.

Israel's insistence on keeping all of Jerusalem and retaining the recently acquired occupied territories caused another war. In October 1973, Syrian and Egyptian armies attacked Israel on Yom Kippur, the holiest day of the Jewish year. Taken by surprise, Israel suffered great loss of life but managed to beat back the attack. Sporadic clashes continued and in 1974, an agreement was signed that resulted in Israel's withdrawal from the Sinai and a United Nations peace-keeping force between Israel and Egypt.

Previously enemies, later friends: Israeli Prime Minister Menachem Begin (left) and President Anwar el-Sadat of Egypt.

ISRAEL TODAY

A breakthrough in the peace process came in 1977 when Egyptian President Anwar el-Sadat stated his willingness to meet with Israeli leaders to settle the Palestine issue. In 1978, United States' President Jimmy Carter held a meeting with Sadat and Israeli Prime Minister Menachem Begin that resulted in a peace treaty. It spelled out Israel's withdrawal from the Sinai Peninsula and eventual Arab self-rule in the West Bank and the Gaza Strip.

Though these were strong signs of progress toward peace in the Middle East, Lebanon, to Israel's north, was involved in a civil war. In addition, the border with Lebanon had been a source of trouble since a branch of the PLO took control of a portion of southern Lebanon. In 1982, ongoing clashes and an assassination attempt on an Israeli ambassador pushed Israel to invade Lebanon in order to attack the PLO. The Israeli army successfully drove out the PLO and helped create a political system led by the Lebanese Maronite Christians, who signed a peace treaty. However, under pressure from Syria, Lebanon canceled the agreement. After strong public opposition, Israel eventually withdrew its forces in 1985.

Israeli Foreign Minister Shimon Peres signing the agreement in Washington on September 13, 1993, giving the Palestinians the right to self-rule in the Gaza Strip and the West Bank town of Jericho. Directly behind him are US President Bill Clinton and PLO Chairman Yasser Arafat.

Two years later, Palestinians in Gaza rioted, causing general civil disobedience and unrest (known as the *Intifada*) throughout Israel's occupied territories. However, a year later, the PLO declared itself an independent state, which was seen as unspoken recognition of Israel's right to exist. This positive step prompted the United States to start low-level peace talks between Israel and the PLO.

In 1991, during the Gulf War, Israel was attacked by missiles from Iraq. Though many missiles were fired at Israel, there were only slight casualties and damage to buildings. Israel wisely chose not to attack Iraq, but instead let a combined force from other countries defeat its enemies. This action earned the country admiration from around the world.

In September 1993, Israel and the PLO signed a peace accord in which Israel would give Palestinians self-government in the Gaza Strip and the West Bank town of Jericho. This agreement was honored on May 13, 1994. The next step in the peace process will be self-rule for the Palestinians in the rest of the West Bank. Israel is also prepared to consider withdrawing its troops from the Golan Heights.

GOVERNMENT

ISRAEL IS A PARLIAMENTARY DEMOCRACY with a unicameral (one-house) legislature. This legislature—known as the Knesset—and the prime minister and the cabinet are responsible for governing Israel.

The president is the head of state, elected by parliament to a five-year term. The president's role is mainly ceremonial, much the same as that of the reigning monarch of the United Kingdom. This official has little governmental power, except to grant pardons and appoint a prime minister and judges to the Supreme Court.

The president also appoints ambassadors and the state comptroller, who oversees budgets and the functions of all public bodies, and performs moral and educational functions. All residents of Israel are eligible to be presidential candidates.

Opposite: **A statue of the menorah, the traditional symbol of Judaism and the Knesset.**

Left: **David Ben-Gurion, Israel's first prime minister, making the Declaration of Independence speech, in 1949.**

The Knesset building in Jerusalem.

THE KNESSET

The Knesset has 120 members who are elected for a maximum of four years; the 120 seats are given in direct ratio to the popular vote. Voters do not elect individuals, but political parties and, subsequently, the candidates they support. The more votes a party gets, the more seats it wins in the parliament.

No party has ever achieved a clear majority in the history of Israeli politics. The system is often criticized because voters have little control over the individuals who obtain these critical seats. However, those who support the system point out that it forces people to vote on issues rather than people.

The Knesset conducts business in a way similar to the British House of Commons, and its voting system is like the ones used in France and Germany. It has unlimited legislative authority, and enactments cannot be vetoed by the prime minister, president, or Supreme Court. It meets weekly, but never comes together on a Friday, Saturday, or Sunday, the holy days for Muslim, Jewish, and Christian members.

BASIC LAWS

The Jewish state has no formal constitution, only a set of basic laws that were enacted with the intention that they would eventually become part of a constitution.

In the early years of statehood, Israeli lawmakers tried to compose a formal document. However, no agreement could be reached. So in 1950, the Knesset decided to gradually acquire a constitution, with the resolution stating that it would grow "chapter by chapter in such a way that each chapter will by itself constitute a fundamental law."

By the late 1980s, there were nine basic laws. These involve areas such as the function of the Knesset, the definition of Israel's borders, the role of the president, the operation of the government, the state economy, the army, the judiciary, elections, and Jerusalem.

There is no procedure to change the laws, although the Knesset can start a new government by simply getting a majority vote. But this is not likely to happen because the government is devoted to a rich tradition of democracy and the exchange of political ideas.

Mounted police in the Arab area of Jerusalem.

THE JUDICIAL SYSTEM

The judicial structure is composed of three courts: military, civil, and religious. Crime is handled by the civil court; marriage and divorce are administered by the religious court; and military matters are overseen by the military court.

Before taking office, judges must pledge allegiance to the state of Israel and take an oath to be neutral and just at all times. In addition, all judges, except those in the religious court, must vow loyalty to the laws of the state.

Laws are borrowed from many areas, including Ottoman and British laws. Special investigative panels have been formed for unusual cases or situations. For example, one was formed after the massacre of Palestinians in Beirut during the 1982 Lebanon War to find and convict those who were responsible for the actions.

The Supreme Court hears appeals from civil and criminal cases. It also hears cases that do not fall directly under the authority of the other courts. The number of justices that make up the Supreme Court is determined by the Knesset. In recent years, there have been 11 justices; a minimum of three must be present to hold a court session.

The Supreme Court is the principal guardian of fundamental rights in Israel and protects individuals from unfair or wrong practices by public agencies and officials. It has authority in almost all areas of Israeli life and functions almost like a formal constitution. Many Israelis consider the Supreme Court the guardian of democracy.

RELIGIOUS COURTS

Religious courts in Israel have authority over personal matters such as marriage, divorce, alimony, and religious wills of members of a religious community. Each major religious community has its own courts, deciding on all

The seat of the Chief Rabbinate of Israel.

matters of their members' personal status and problems. If people of different religions are involved in a legal dispute, the president of the Supreme Court determines which court will have authority.

District courts can also have authority in personal legal matters if all parties involved agree on their participation.

Within the state of Israel, there are Jewish Rabinnical Courts, Muslim Religious Courts, Christian Religious Courts, and Druze Courts.

Tel Aviv City Hall.

THE CABINET

The cabinet, consisting of the prime minister and a number of ministers, is Israel's central political power and the top policy-making body. The prime minister must be a member of the Knesset, but this is not required of the other cabinet ministers. The Knesset confirms the cabinet after the prime minister submits a list of names and a detailed report of the policies and fundamental principles of the cabinet.

The cabinet can be dissolved if the prime minister dies, if the Knesset officially reprimands it (known as "passing a censure"), or if it resigns as a group. Individuals can resign from the cabinet without disbanding it, but if the prime minister resigns, the whole cabinet must go with him or her.

Cabinet posts are divided among the various political parties or coalitions of the smaller ones, usually in proportion to the strength of the various parties.

LOCAL GOVERNMENT

Israel is divided into six administrative districts, each of which has a commissioner. Towns and cities with more than 20,000 people are run by municipal corporations, whereas smaller towns are run by local councils. Villages are collectively administered by regional councils.

There are 46 municipalities, 143 local councils, and 54 regional councils representing 700 villages, some of which are mainly Druze or Arab. All local government authorities are chosen in elections like the rest of the government.

The local government provides basic services such as water, drainage, roads, parks, and social assistance, as well as sports, cultural, health, and educational facilities. To provide such services, it gets funds from a municipal tax, where the rates and budgets are authorized by the Ministry of the Interior.

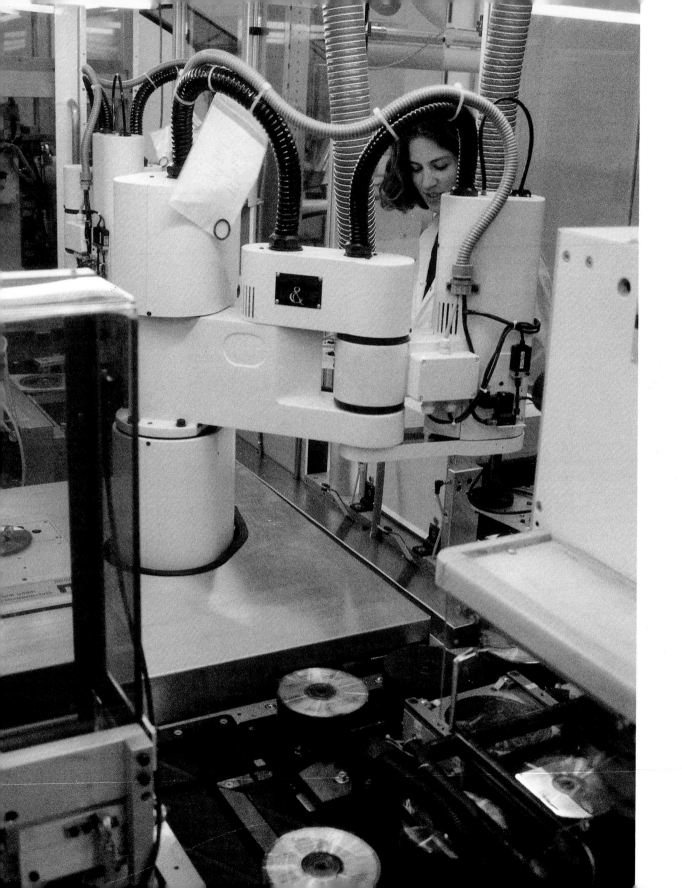

ECONOMY

ISRAEL HAS HAD TWO DISTINCT ECONOMIC PERIODS: the first from 1948 to 1972, and the second from 1973 to the present.

The beginning of the first period was extremely difficult. As a new state, Israel had little or no economic framework or reserves, and limited natural resources and public services. A strong factor influencing the economic state of the country was that many established Arabs left at the very same time needy Jewish refugees entered.

Israel faced no small task. It had to produce and supply food for its new arrivals, provide housing and clothing, and set up civil service, monetary, and economic systems. In addition, the neighboring Arab countries blocked free trade with it.

Opposite: **A computer disk factory in West Galilee.**

Left: **Buildings in the business district of Tel Aviv.**

ECONOMIC GROWTH

Israel overcame its early economic problems partly because of outside investment and foreign aid. It received gifts, loans, and grants from the United States, donations from Jews around the world, and reparation funds from West Germany for crimes against Jews during World War II. That, combined with the resourcefulness of the Israelis, provided the great push for the country's economic growth. From the late 1940s until the mid-1970s, Israeli goods and services increased 10% annually, which was unequaled by any other country in the free world for the same period.

The second economic period began in 1973. There were periods of strong growth followed by stagnation and high unemployment. Nonetheless, in the 1970s, Israel had achieved a standard of living close to that of Western countries. The 1973 Yom Kippur War, however, created new economic woes. But the United States continued to provide aid, which further reduced the burden.

By 1990, the goods and services produced totaled $50 billion. Inflation was rampant, however, and strict price controls were set on essential goods. Tariffs were placed on imported goods, and a tax on travel was set up. These efforts proved successful as inflation came down to a more manageable level.

Due to its limited natural resources, Israel continues to rely on imports. It still imports far more than it exports, creating a large trade deficit.

The government plays a significant role in Israel's economy; it owns and operates the postal, telegraph, and telephone systems as well as the railways. It is also involved in public works.

Israel's national income comes from manufacturing and mining, trade, construction, service industries, agriculture, and transportation and communications.

Workers making bricks to be used in construction.

THE LABOR FORCE AND UNIONS

Nearly all workers in Israel are members of a union. Women make up nearly one-third of the total labor force.

Although there are four labor unions, the most important one is Histadrut, or the General Federation of Labor. Nearly 70% of all union workers belong to its trade union division, which owns many of Israel's businesses. It is the second largest employer in the country.

Histadrut was created by the Zionist workers' movement in the early part of this century. In addition to its labor union, it operates social service programs, develops industrial projects, and provides free education programs.

All types of workers make up Histadrut: professional, technical, agricultural, civil service, and industrial. It is estimated that 40% of Israel's population belongs to Histadrut. This is because the families of members are entitled to membership, as are Arab workers.

The other three unions in Israel represent approximately 250,000 workers. Two of these, Poale I Agudat Israel ("POH-ahl-leh ah-goo-DAHT ISS-rah-ell") and Ha-Poel Ha-Mizrachi ("ah-poh-ELL ah-miz-rah-HEE"), are religious unions that occasionally team up with Histadrut on certain projects. The other is the National Labor Federation.

AGRICULTURE

Agricultural expansion was a focus of the early Zionist movement in Palestine because it was the way to work and restore the ancestral

homeland. The settlers created the kibbutzim (collective farms) to fulfill their dreams in the "land of milk and honey." After 1948, however, it became an economic necessity to develop other sources for food that previously had been imported from Arab countries.

Much of Israel's agricultural land is the property of the state. Although only 20% of the land can be farmed, the imagination and skills of the people paved the way for success. Marshland was drained and rocks moved to reveal usable farmland. Where there was no water, irrigation systems and greenhouse-like arrangements were built. The result of all this is that the amount of farmable land increased. Today, nearly all of Israel's food needs are met by its agricultural production, and it even produces enough to be exported.

In spite of all this, just 5% of Israel's labor force is engaged in agriculture. Major agricultural products include citrus fruits, cotton, vegetables, grain, dairy products, and beef. Its main exports are citrus fruits and cut flowers.

Plastic farming, a new type of desert farming, is practiced near the Dead Sea.

A young Arab selling clothes in Jerusalem's Old City.

INDUSTRY

Nearly one-third of Israel's workers are involved in industry, and it is estimated that industry generates nearly 30% of the national income.

The greatest concentration of heavy industry is in the Haifa area, while Tel Aviv is home to light industries such as textile manufacturing and food processing. Shoes, pencils, and printed items are produced around Jerusalem.

The electronics industry is providing a great boost to the Israeli economy, employing nearly 12% of the work force. Most of the electronic equipment produced is used domestically for defense or communications.

Another prospering industry is cutting, polishing, and trading diamonds, though the gems are mined in other countries. This practice originated in the town of Netanya. Now the center of this activity is Tel Aviv, where the Israel Diamond Exchange and Bourse is among the world's largest diamond markets.

46

MINERAL WEALTH

The Dead Sea provides large quantities of potash, bromine, and other salt deposits. Potash and copper production is also flourishing. The desert also yields valuable minerals: there is granite and phosphates in the Negev, and minerals for making glass and porcelain are found near Beersheba. Oil is found in the northern Negev and northeast of Beersheba.

FISHING

Fishing has developed into an important industry, though the Israelis must send boats as far as the Ethiopian coast and the Atlantic Ocean to fish. This is because there are not a lot of fish along the Mediterranean and Red Sea coasts, or in the Sea of Galilee. About one-third of the fish netted by Israeli fishing boats are freshwater varieties raised in artificial ponds, many of which are part of a kibbutz.

A tour bus in the Negev Desert waiting for tourists who are visiting the mountain fortress of Masada, which is in the background.

FOOD FROM THE DESERT

In the early 1900s, when the Zionist movement was starting, Jewish settlers encountered a poverty-stricken land of sand dunes, swamps, and vast desert. Their first order of business was to prepare the land for settlement and fully utilize all its natural resources.

This remains a priority for Israel. Right in the middle of the Negev Desert, where the temperature can exceed 120°F and there is an annual rainfall of less than an inch, more than 250 agricultural settlements thrive. Using one of its most abundant resources—salt water—Israel has revolutionized management of land and water resources in desert environments. What makes this feat so great is that the crops are not only irrigated through underground water beneath the desert, they are irrigated with salt water!

Because desalination (removal of salt from salt water) is very costly, the developers of the Negev settlement cultivated plants that did not soak up salt. It took scientists six years of experimentation to strike a correct balance of water nutrients, salt, and sun. The process, known as brackish-water agriculture, has made great strides. It has perfected the Negev tomato, which is quite popular in Europe because of its rich taste and ability to stay fresh for about a month. In addition, it has enabled Israel to export approximately 50% of its annual harvest.

The amount of cotton produced in Israel now surpasses that of Egypt and the states of California and Arizona. Peanut production is more than four times that of the states of Georgia and West Virginia. It is hoped that in a few years, the Negev will be the main producer of winter vegetables for Europe.

TOURISM

A vital source of income and foreign currency for Israel has been tourism. Because of its historical sites and places of religious importance, by the mid-1980s the industry was earning more than $1 billion.

Since then, however, there has been a decline in the number of people traveling to Israel (and the Middle East in general) because of security difficulties and the weakening of the American dollar against European currencies. At its peak, tourism brought more than one million visitors to Israel every year. Approximately 20% were from the United States.

ISRAELIS

THE ESTIMATED POPULATION OF ISRAEL in mid-1993 was 5.3 million people. Of that figure, 80% were Jews and the remainder Arabs.

Recent world events have had an impact on the population statistics of Israel: the breakup of the Soviet Union resulted in more than 340,000 immigrants coming to Israel between mid-1989 and the end of 1991. Famine in Ethiopia in the mid-1980s resulted in an airlift of 10,000 Ethiopian Jews to Israel. And in the spring of 1991, Operation Solomon, an airlift of 14,500 additional Ethiopians, was carried out just before the Ethiopian government fell to rebel forces.

The Law of Return, which grants citizenship to any Jew who emigrates to Israel, ensures that there is a place for these people.

Opposite: **Arab children in front of a Turkish tower in Acre.**

Left: **People waiting for a bus in Jerusalem.**

JEWISH ETHNIC GROUPS

The Diaspora (the dispersion of Jews dating back to the 2nd century) was the most significant influence on the creation of different ethnic groups within Judaism. These Jews were scattered throughout the world and they lacked a homeland. Though they clung to the study and observance of Jewish religious scriptures and attempted to follow the laws and rituals of the religion, they adopted many attitudes of their new lands.

Indeed the Jews of Israel share a common identity through Judaism, but they are not an identical people. Coming to the Holy Land from more than 100 countries, they bring numerous languages and customs.

There are two dominant Jewish ethnic groups in Israel. The Ashkenazim ("AHSH-kuh-NAH-zim") are Jews from northern and eastern Europe, and the Sephardim ("suh-FAR-dim") are from Aegean, Mediterranean, Balkan, and Middle Eastern backgrounds.

The Ashkenazim were among the leaders of the Zionist movement who brought with them the Western lifestyles that set the pace for Israel's cultural and intellectual development. The Sephardim, on the other hand, made up the majority of immigrants after 1950. Many were from small villages in North Africa and had attitudes and lifestyles that were quite similar to those of the Arab minority in Israel.

Another major difference between these two groups was their view of Israel. The Sephardim saw life in Israel as delivery from exile and the fulfillment of a biblical prophecy. The Ashkenazim had suffered persecution in their former homelands and hoped to find political and religious freedom in the Jewish state.

Until recently, the Sephardim placed less emphasis on political matters than did the Ashkenazim, who remain Israel's more influential group. The Likud Party's 1988 electoral victory is closely aligned to the Sephardic Jews' somewhat recent involvement in politics, and it is seen as a positive step toward lessening the social and economic gaps between these two groups.

It is ironic that this division exists, for the main aim of Zionism was to eliminate the Diaspora and unite the Jews as one people in a uniform society without class division.

An Israeli police officer.

53

Children of Ethiopian immigrants with Israeli volunteer teachers.

IMMIGRATION TRENDS: THE ALIYOT

The word *aliyah* (plural *aliyot*), which literally means "going up," refers to the immigration of Jews to the land of Israel. Five major periods of *aliyot* have contributed to the development of Israel's people.

The First Aliyah, from 1882 to 1903, brought 25,000 Jews, mostly fleeing Russia. Their arrival doubled the Jewish population in Palestine and caused the first clash between the Ashkenazim and the Sephardim. The new arrivals were less religious and more interested in establishing a Jewish nation, while the Palestinian Jews were not political but quite religious. During this *aliyah*, several thousand Jews from Yemen also arrived.

The Second and Third Aliyot, from 1904 to 1923, brought 76,000 Jews mainly from Russia and Poland. These immigrants succeeded in creating the kibbutzim, cooperative villages (moshavim), the labor federation (Histadrut), and Israel's education system. Approximately 349,000 central European immigrants came in the Fourth and Fifth Aliyot, from 1924 to 1939, mostly to escape Nazism. A large percentage were professionals and businessmen, and this group contributed greatly to the industrial, cultural, and commercial development of the country.

Immigrants from 1948 to 1969 numbered 1.25 million. Half were from Asia and North Africa. These Sephardic Jews were outwardly accepted into Israeli society, but the serious rift between the two Jewish groups was gaining a strong foothold.

Today, as the country absorbs thousands of Soviet Jews in addition to thousands of recent Ethiopian arrivals, the character of the nation will undergo further changes.

The entrance to a *shuk* ("shook") or open market, a favorite place for immigrant Jews to meet and shop.

Arab women shopping in a Beersheba market.

ISRAELI ARABS

The Israeli Arab population, more than three-quarters of whom are Sunni Muslims, has remained concentrated in the northern and Haifa districts since 1948. Approximately two-thirds of Israel's Arab citizenry live in urban areas, and are mainly employed in construction and industry rather than the traditional agricultural occupations.

The standard of living for Arabs in Israel has improved since Israel's statehood. As citizens, the Arabs share in the health, welfare, and education systems. The infant death rates have declined since the end of the British mandate period.

Nonetheless, the Arabs make up an ethnic and religious minority in a country where they were previously a majority. Though Arab citizens have voting rights and government representation at both the local and national levels, they are excluded from military service and there are some government jobs that they cannot hold. They also have less access to land ownership and certain types of government funding than Jews. Increasing Arab sympathy for the Palestine Liberation Organization is also causing resentment and ill feelings between the Jewish majority and the Arab minority.

Israeli Arabs generally remain loyal to their cultural, religious, and political backgrounds. Like the Jews, even though they share a common ethnic identity, the Arabs are made up of different groups of people. This prevents them from uniting as a single pressure group that can have an effective impact on the Jewish majority.

THE BEDOUINS

The Bedouin population in Israel represents some 40 tribal groups living primarily in the Negev Desert in southern Israel. Because they are nomads who pitch their goat's hair tents wherever they can find an area to graze their animals, it is difficult to determine the exact number of Bedouins. But reliable estimates put the number of Israeli Bedouins at 29,000.

The Bedouins eat, sleep, travel, and trade in much the same way that they did 1,500 years ago. Along with their camels, they are well-known for having conquered the desert. They live mostly off camel, goat, and sheep herding, and are considered good traders. They are also great hosts; whenever they have visitors, they always give their very best food.

The Bedouins have an uncanny tracking ability; they are known as the best desert trackers in the world. They are able to find traces of people or animals in the sand, tell if the animal had been running, or whether a man or woman was carrying equipment.

This very special skill has made Bedouins very valuable to the Israeli army, especially for guarding the borders. They are among those few Israeli Arabs who can volunteer to serve in the army, and are always called upon to track down enemy troops who have broken through Israel's border defenses.

The Bedouins pride themselves on their capacity for hospitality and concern for people. However, their code of conduct does not see their habit of raiding other tribes' livestock as something that is wrong.

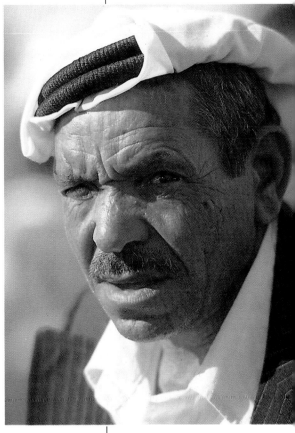

An Israeli Bedouin.

A Druze from the village of Boukata in the Golan Heights.

THE DRUZE

The Druze are an Arab sect that established its own branch of Islam in the 11th century. One of the most fascinating things about this group is that they have kept their religion a secret, though it is believed that parts of Jewish and Christian tenets have been absorbed into the Druze faith. This sect lives by its principles and merely wants to be left undisturbed.

The Druze live in the area where Syria, Lebanon, and Israel meet. They number 33,000 in Israel, many living in the Golan Heights, and make their living by farming. The Israeli Druze have adapted to Israeli society better than any other Arab group and, unlike most Arabs, are pro-Israel. For years, the Druze have been drafted into the army, and they have representatives in the Knesset.

The one exception to this friendly Jewish-Druze relationship involves the Druze of the Golan Heights. Though these Arabs have been Israeli citizens since the 1967 war, they feel they are unwilling victims of the Israeli-Syrian dispute, so they chose not to vote and are not drafted into the army. Unlike other Arabs in the occupied territories, however, they do not openly oppose Israel.

OTHER MINORITIES

There are also small communities of Karaites (15,000 people) in the towns of Ashdod, Beersheba, and Ramla; Circassians (4,000) in two villages in Galilee; and Samaritans (550) in the towns of Holon and Shechem.

THE TEN LOST TRIBES OF ISRAEL

Israel's most recent wave of Sephardic immigrants, the Ethiopian Jews, have quite different religious customs from the other Jewish groups that have returned to the Holy Land—so different that their "Jewishness" was a topic of conversation among Israel's chief rabbis. The differences are the result of the Ethiopians' isolation from mainstream Judaism.

What caused that isolation? According to Jewish history, 12 ancient tribes lived in Palestine. After years of fighting among themselves, the land was divided into the kingdom of Israel in the north, where 10 tribes lived, and the kingdom of Judah in the south, home to the remaining two tribes.

In 722 B.C., the kingdom of Israel was conquered by the Assyrians, and its inhabitants exiled to "Halah and Habor by the river Gozan, and in the cities of Medes." These 10 tribes were never seen again, and they are known as the Ten Lost Tribes of Israel.

Biblical prophets Isaiah, Jeremiah, and Ezekiel promised that the lost tribes would eventually be reunited with the rest of the nation, and this has kept the memory and search for the tribes alive. Thus, many think that the return of the Ethiopian Jews to Israel is a 10% fulfillment of that prophecy; the black Jews are believed to be the descendants of King Solomon and the queen of Sheba.

Throughout history, attempts have been made to explain how the tribes disappeared and to discover them. An 1871 book even presented 47 "proofs" that the British were part of the Ten Lost Tribes.

The search goes on. For the last two decades, an organization called Amishav has been dedicated to finding lost Jews from around the world. The group's mission is to return these people to the land, for according to biblical prophecy, the Messiah will come only after all 12 tribes return to Israel.

LIFESTYLE

A FUNDAMENTAL PRINCIPLE of the state of Israel is that every Jew has the right to settle there. The Law of Return gives legal status to this principle; it grants automatic citizenship to any Jew who wants it. Also guaranteed is freedom of worship. As a result of this, there are many lifestyles within this tiny nation. The range of lifestyles among the Israelis does not fall along religious lines; the life of the Ultraorthodox Jew no more resembles the life of the secular Jew of the kibbutz than it does the nomadic Bedouin or the mysterious Druze.

Israeli society is a kaleidoscope of customs, traditions, and beliefs. The ways in which these numerous groups conduct their lives and interact with one another presents a very interesting picture.

Opposite: **Inside the Dizengof Center in Tel Aviv.**

Left: **Modern housing for the citizens of Jerusalem.**

A gathering of Jewish people.

ZIONISM

The goal of Zionism was to establish a homeland where Jews would not be a minority. By attaining this independence, Jews would no longer be dependent on others for their safety and well-being. Also, the early pioneers felt that no matter where the Jews lived, they would be spiritual prisoners of a non-Jewish society—meaning, they would always question what the non-Jewish world might say about their every move.

Zionist pioneers felt that making the Jewish people citizens of their own land would ease anti-Semitism and give Jews spiritual and emotional freedom.

Though the Zionist movement got under way in the late 1800s, the dream was realized only about 50 years later when Israel declared its statehood in 1948. Yet since that time, Israel has been isolated from its neighbors and in ever-present danger of total destruction.

JUDAISM IN EVERYDAY LIFE

Judaism is the unifying force and basis for the establishment of the state of Israel. The bond among Jews strengthens during times of Arab opposition. Nonetheless, a deep division exists among Jews and it continues to be an important issue.

The major division among Israelis is between religious Jews and secular Jews, and over the separation of synagogue and government. It is estimated that more than 75% of Israel's Jewish population considers itself secular. While it would seem that the religious minority would not play a significant role in Israeli day-to-day life, quite the opposite is true. Religious groups form political parties, and even a small group can exert considerable political influence.

Religious Jews feel that because Israel is a Jewish state, it should be based on Jewish customs and laws, and that the secular part affecting Jewish life should be checked. They maintain that Jewish tradition is what held the Jewish people together during centuries of separation, and it is what led to the establishment of Israel.

An Orthodox Jew praying by the Wailing Wall.

On the other hand, secular Israelis insist that religious involvement should be a matter of personal choice and that in a democracy, separation of Judaism and government is important.

Furthermore, because Judaism is considered not just a religion but a way of life, secular Jews believe the imposing of ritual and tradition by the religious groups would prevent them from enjoying the religious freedom that is guaranteed in Israel.

LIFE ON THE KIBBUTZ

The kibbutz is one of the original contributions of the Jewish settlers in modern Israel. A kibbutz is a community where people choose to live and work together, growing their own food and sharing everything. All members are equal and women are freed from household chores so that they can participate in the successful running of the community.

Members of Kibbutz Gezer picking melons.

The first kibbutz was formed in 1909 when seven pioneers working near the Sea of Galilee asked the Jewish National Fund to allow them to farm a piece of land. These early settlers felt that working the land would bind the Jews to their new homeland. Kibbutz Degania was the result of this idea, and the kibbutz has been a working institution for more than 80 years.

Today, there are more than 800 kibbutzim (the plural of kibbutz), ranging in size from 100 members to as many as 2,000. Land is leased to the kibbutzniks (residents of the kibbutz) for a 49-year period, at which time the lease can be renewed. Kibbutz Degania ("day-GAH-nee-uh") continues today as one of the most successful settlements in Israel. It became so large that it had to be divided into two: Degania Alef ("AH-lef," or A) and Degania Bet ("BET," or B).

The kibbutz provides all the needs of its residents, and no one is paid for his or her work. Kibbutzniks eat in communal dining rooms; they get their clothing from the community's shop, and have it washed at a communal laundry or repaired at a communal tailor shop. All cars and trucks on the kibbutz are owned by the community.

Each kibbutz strives to be fair to every member. Decisions are made at weekly meetings, and everything that is produced and earned is shared equally with all members. Committees are elected to deal with certain management issues.

There is one aspect of family life that really sets kibbutzniks apart from other families. In many villages, children live separately from their parents in houses with other children of their age groups. In the evenings, they spend time with their fathers and mothers in the parents' living quarters. In other kibbutzim, however, residents feel that family life is central to Jewish culture, and the family lives together in private kibbutz housing. All kibbutzim youngsters, however, have their own jobs and responsibilities, and often have to take care of crops. They attend schools that are independent of the Israeli school system, where the schedule includes certain hours on the farm and teachers labor with students in maintaining the land.

While farming is still very important on the kibbutz, many kibbutzim engage in other industries such as textiles, furniture production, and even telecommunications equipment production. Economic realities have caused many kibbutzim to consider non-traditional methods of making a profit to survive. Some have opened day-care centers for children from neighboring towns, or have begun charging outsiders admission for the use of the kibbutz swimming pool. Some have even hired non-kibbutznik managers to keep the operations profitable.

There are also a number of religious kibbutzim that choose the traditional principles of labor, equality, and communal living, but combine them with an organized way of life according to Judaism. Dealing with daily chores of the farm on the Sabbath has required the religious kibbutzniks to come up with creative solutions, like automatically regulated milking equipment.

Though only 4% of Israelis live on the kibbutzim, Israelis consider the kibbutz life admirable, and kibbutzniks are treated with great respect. They make up about 14% of army officers, and many serve in the Knesset.

"The kibbutz isn't a party, but a way of life. It's broader than a party. Politics for the kibbutz members means the sum of their activities to affect the world around them."

— Moshe (Musa) Harif, leader of the United Kibbutz Movement

Arab children going to school in the Old City section of Jerusalem.

EDUCATION

Israeli law states that primary education should focus on "the values of Jewish culture and the achievements of science; on love of the homeland and devotion to the state and the Jewish people; on training in agricultural work and handicraft; on fulfillment of pioneering principles; and on the aspiration to a society built on freedom, equality, tolerance, mutual assistance, and love of mankind."

Free education is a cornerstone of democracy in the state of Israel, and it is a prime national concern. Approximately 8% of the annual budget is devoted to education. In Israel, education is compulsory and free for children (Jews and Arabs alike) between the ages of five and 16. The system includes kindergarten (the purpose is to ensure that all students know Hebrew), six-year primary schools, three-year junior high schools, and three-year high schools. After high school, students take an exam to determine if they can go on to college. University education is usually pursued after military service.

The government offers three types of schools: secular (without religious connections), religious (which devote attention to religious laws, prayers, and the Talmud), and schools for Israeli Arabs. Private religious schools, run by independent orthodox organizations, are also available. In these institutions, boys and girls are educated in separate classes. After graduating from these schools at the age of 14, boys generally enter a *yeshiva* ("yeh-SHI-veh"), or religious college, to become rabbis.

Students attend school six days a week. In primary school, they study Hebrew, the Bible, geography, science, mathematics, crafts, art and music, history, and physical education. English classes start in the fifth grade, and Arabic is often taught as a third language.

An Israeli teacher with her class.

Children from Arab villages and Bedouin camps can go to school too. For the Bedouins, there are field schools that move with the population. Arabic is the language of instruction in all Israeli Arab schools, and Hebrew is taught as a second language. Most teachers in these schools are Arabs, and emphasis is placed on Arabic history and culture, and Islam. Textbooks used are direct Arabic translations of the Hebrew texts used in Jewish schools. In the occupied territories, schools are under the authority of the local municipality.

Post-secondary education is open to anyone who is qualified. There are 12 institutes of higher education in Israel. Hebrew University in Jerusalem and Tel Aviv University educate approximately 40,000 students between them. Others include the University of the Negev, Haifa University, and Bar Ilan University. The Technion in Haifa and the Weizmann Institute in Rehovot are well-known technology and science schools.

Young Israeli soldiers taking a rest on the sidewalk.

THE ARMY

The Israeli army (also known as the Israel Defense Forces or IDF) plays an important part in the lives of all young Israelis. The average sabra grows up knowing that once he or she reaches the age of 17 or 18, military service is next.

All Israeli citizens must serve, except those who are handicapped or extremely religious. Though military service is compulsory, Israelis look upon it with pride and joy. Men serve for three years, women for two. In addition, men must serve four weeks in the active reserves each year until they reach the age of 55, whereas unmarried women remain in the reserves until they are 34.

The military also serves a social function in Israel. Because Jews who emigrate to Israel are granted immediate citizenship, the new arrival's first duty is military service. While in the army, they learn to speak and read Hebrew, study the history and geography of their new country, and are taught everything about their citizenship.

Only after completing military service can Israelis pursue higher education. Many, however, get a head start by seeking army jobs in fields that they would like to enter later on. Becoming an officer is also beneficial; the most successful executives, managers, and government employees were officers during their military service, so the youth generally take their time in the IDF very seriously.

ULPAN

The *ulpan* ("ool-PAHN") is an institute specially designed to teach immigrants about the cultures of Israel and to offer intensive Hebrew language lessons. There are several types of *ulpan*: for example, the residential *ulpan* is popular among professionals and meets for five hours a day for five months; the kibbutzim *ulpan* for younger people has students working for four hours and studying the rest of the day.

Students attend day *ulpan* once a week, while the popular *ulpan* meets either in the morning or evening.

YOUTH MOVEMENTS

Israeli youth organizations are active as extracurricular education and recreation for children and teenagers between the ages of 10 and 16. Almost every young Israeli is a member of a youth movement. The largest group has ties with the Histadrut Labor Organization, serving as a type of junior trade union that provides vocational education and union benefits.

The Israel Scout Federation meets weekly for games, cultural activities, and educational programs. Members wear khaki uniforms and colorful kerchiefs, and leaders stress the pioneering spirit and the benefits of living off the land. This group is associated with the International Scouting Movement. Bene Akiva is the largest religious youth movement and is closely connected with the kibbutz movement.

"The army represents a symbol of duty, and as long as women are not equal in this duty, they have not attained equality."

—David Ben-Gurion, Israel's first prime minister.

A Circassian father and his children.

THE FAMILY

The family has always been important in Jewish life. Though many different ethnic groups, lifestyles, and attitudes make up the Israeli population, one thing that remains the same is the importance of the close-knit family unit.

For most Israeli families, regardless of whether they are secular or religious, kibbutznik or city-dweller, dinner time is usually the focal point of the family experience, for with the exception of the Sabbath, it is often the only time that the entire family can be together.

Because of the religious atmosphere in Israel, most families celebrate the Jewish festivals as holidays, and they cherish this time as "quality" time with the family.

MARRIAGE

In Judaism, marriage is considered the ideal human state; it is the basic social institution that God established at the time of creation. Jews agree with the Bible's statement that marriage is for companionship, self-fulfillment, and producing children. According to Orthodox Jewish law, marriage consists of two acts called *kiddushin* ("ki-DOO-shin") and *nissuin* ("ni-SOO-in"). *Kiddushin* is the legal "receiving" of the bride by the groom. The groom hands over an object of value to the bride in the presence of two witnesses and says, "Behold, you are consecrated unto me with this ring, according to the law of Moses and Israel." By this act, he states his intention to reserve the bride for himself. By accepting the item of value (usually a ring), the bride indicates that she agrees.

In the *nissuin* ceremony, the mothers of the bride and groom lead the bride to the huppah ("koo-PAH," bridal canopy), which symbolizes the groom's house, and blessings are said. The groom is accompanied to the huppah by the fathers of the bride and groom. The ceremony is customarily performed in the presence of a *minyan* ("MIN-yehn," a group of 10 men). After the bride and groom drink from a goblet of wine, the groom places the ring on the index finger of the bride's right hand, and repeats what he said during the *kiddushin*. Seven marriage blessings are recited over another goblet of wine, and the groom concludes the ceremony by crushing a glass under his right foot. (The breaking of glass signifies the mourning of the destruction of the temple in Jerusalem in A.D. 70.) After the ceremony, the couple is led to a private room in which they spend time together. It is only after this private time that they are considered husband and wife.

A bride and groom posing for pictures.

GET (DIVORCE CEREMONY)

In Judaism, when a married couple no longer shares a loving relationship, it is acceptable to get a divorce. Marriage and divorce are seen as acts of free will. Divorces, nevertheless, sadden and deeply hurt everybody involved.

Babies in the nursery at Kibbutz Netiv Halamed-Hey.

In Israel, divorce is handled through the Jewish Rabinnical Court, because the laws of the state are the traditional laws of marriage and divorce. The *get* ("geht") is the bill of divorce, the document releasing the woman from her marriage. The *get* document itself is written on heavy white paper. Special ink is used to write the text— ink that cannot be erased—so that no changes can be introduced after it is written.

According to Jewish law, only after the *get* is delivered into the hands of the wife does the divorce take place. At the ceremony, the husband and wife meet before the *beth din* ("beht-DIN," rabbinical court), and the husband hands the wife the 12-line *get* document. Until she holds the document, the divorce is not finalized. After taking the piece of paper, the wife either takes a few symbolic steps or walks into another room. At that point, she is once again an unmarried woman.

BIRTH RITUALS

Historically, there is greater joy at the birth of a boy than of a girl. Jewish birth rituals differ for boys and girls.

Though the child of a Jewish mother is Jewish at birth, a boy enters Judaism on his eighth day of life, the day of his *brit* ("brit," or ritual circumcision, sometimes pronounced "briss"). The *brit* is a symbol of a

THE BEDOUIN COFFEE RITUAL

Bedouins take pride in their hospitality above almost all else. Most often, the sheikh (leader) receives the camp's guest. If the sheikh is wealthy, the meal will be filling; if the guest is important, there will almost surely be bread served with butter, at the very least. And no matter who the guest is, there will always be coffee.

It is customary to serve a thick, bitter Arab coffee both before and after a meal. The more important the gathering, the more detailed the coffee-making ritual. Coffee making is a solemn duty that is handled by the host himself, especially if only a poor quality of coffee is served. (An influential sheikh may designate a favorite servant or trusted person to prepare the coffee.)

The Bedouin starts by making the fire. He then prepares the equipment and materials; four coffee pots are required. Three of the pots are fire-blackened, while the fourth is shiny and bright. It is from the shiny one that the coffee is served.

The coffee beans are roasted, cooled, and pounded with a pestle. (Bedouins love the pinging sound of the pestle grinding against the mortar.) The ground coffee is poured into the previous day's coffee, and boiled water is added. After the whole brew is heated to boiling point again, cardamom seeds are added for flavor. At this point, the coffee is poured into one of the blackened pots, and then into the shiny pot to allow the grounds to settle. A piece of hemp is placed at the spout to serve as a strainer, and the drink is served.

When the guest has finished, the person signals that he or she has had enough by shaking the empty cup with six shakes of the wrist. The Bedouin host then takes the cup and, if necessary, fills it for another guest awaiting the beloved beverage.

boy's joining the community of Israel. A *mohel* ("maw-HELL"), who is a ritual circumciser, performs the ceremony, which generally takes place at home in the presence of at least 10 people. Godparents are officially involved in the *brit*; the godfather (usually one of the grandfathers) who holds the baby is designated the *sandak* ("sahn-DAHK") and the god-mother who hands the baby to him is the *sandakit* ("sahn-DAH-kit"). Relatives and friends attend the *brit*, and a celebration takes place immediately after the ceremony.

There are no initiation rites for girls, though modern Jews feel strongly that some should be adopted for them. Girls are named in the synagogue in a blessing ceremony that the father receives on the Sabbath after the child's birth. In some synagogues, the baby's name may be inscribed on a parchment to mark the occasion of her naming.

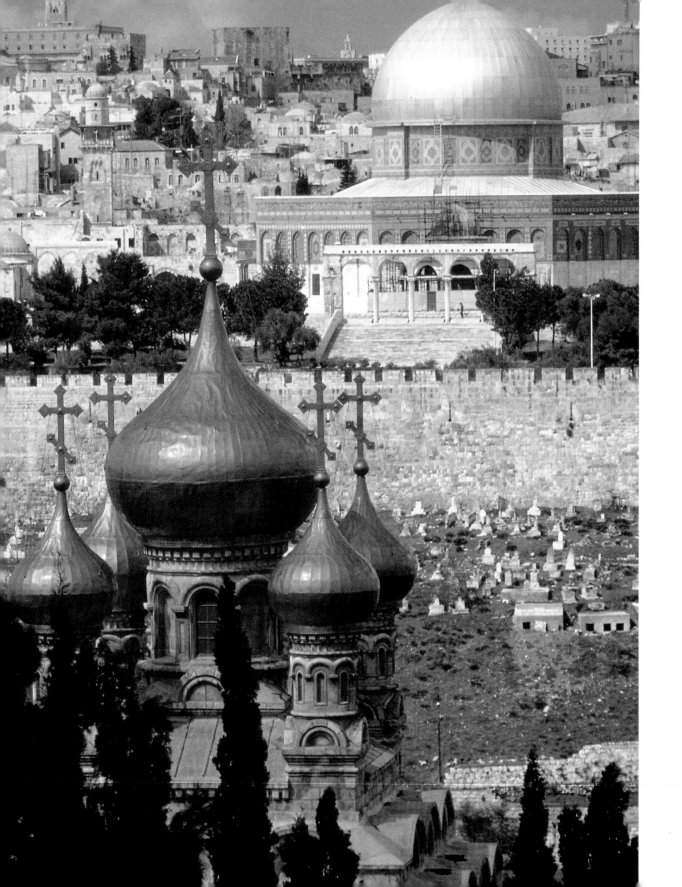

RELIGION

THE DECLARATION OF INDEPENDENCE of the state of Israel guarantees full freedom of worship and the safety of the holy places of all religions. And because Jerusalem has a key role in the development of three of the world's major religions, many different religious traditions are observed in Israel. In the holy cities of the Koran and the Bible, a sense of struggle and passion can almost be felt in the air.

Judaism is the dominant religion in Israel, and it is difficult to separate it from all aspects of life there. It influences the political structure of the government and is the basis for its very nationhood.

No less alive, however, is the zeal of the Muslims, Christians, Druze, and Baha'is.

Opposite: **Jerusalem, the city of three great faiths. Here, the spirals of a church look upon the Dome of the Rock.**

Left: **The menorah engraved into a slab of basalt taken from one of many ancient Jewish synagogues. This slab of stone dates back to the 2nd century A.D.**

JUDAISM

In Judaism, the same basic prayer book, with certain slight changes, and identical weekly readings from the Bible, are in use throughout the world.

"Hear, O Israel, the Lord our God, the Lord is One."

This prayer is the fundamental message of Judaism. It refers to the covenant, or sacred agreement, that Jews will worship only one God and obey His laws. There is no priestly class between God and humanity, therefore Jews can appeal to God for help and praise Him directly.

In Judaism, it is a person's relationship with God that is stressed. The rabbi is the person in the community who is responsible for religious education, guidance, and services in the synagogue. His or her position does not involve special privileges. Rabbis interpret Jewish law and guide the spiritual lives of the people.

In the covenant, which is in the first five books of the Bible (also known as the Torah), God chose the descendants of Abraham to bring knowledge and acceptance of Him to the world. Through this acceptance, the Torah says, all of humanity can have a place in heaven.

The Talmud, another collection of authoritative ancient writings, combines with the Torah to form the religious laws that govern the lives of the Jewish people. These laws include ideas about the equality and rights of all people, personal morality, and personal freedom.

Judaism is a historical religion that focuses on the works of God throughout the past, present, and future rather than on fixed formulas of belief. The focus on the past is through the study of the Bible; the present through living according to Jewish laws; the future in anticipation of the coming Messiah.

Jewish laws are primarily concerned with moral values, teaching that people must be fair and kind to others, and that they should live a good life for the sake of being a good human being. The primary goal of Jewish law is the welfare of society.

BRANCHES OF JUDAISM

Until the 19th century, there was only one approach to Jewish religious tradition, and Judaism was practiced in the way that is referred to today as Orthodox Judaism. Now, other branches of Judaism have come about: Reform, Conservative, and Reconstructionist.

Orthodox means "the right way." People who adhere to this form of Judaism fully accept God's word as it was revealed to Moses in the Torah. Orthodox Jews strictly adhere to the Talmud and later laws of rabbis.

Strict observance of the Sabbath, *kashrut* ("KAHSH-root") or dietary law, and the Jewish holy days are characteristics of Orthodox Judaism. Synagogue services are conducted exclusively in Hebrew. Men are required to wear head coverings and prayer shawls during worship. Married women wear head coverings at all times as evidence of modesty. Men and women are separated during worship in an Orthodox synagogue.

Reform Judaism rejects many of the practices and beliefs of Orthodox Judaism, including the authority of the Talmud and dietary laws. The Reform movement began in Germany in the early 1800s when some Jews felt that they needed to lead their lives in a way that was closer to the lifestyles of the non-Jewish people around them.

In Reform Judaism, head coverings are optional, and women and men worship together. Women can even become rabbis. The religious service is usually conducted in the native language of the worshipers (in the United States, for example, English is used frequently in the service).

Conservative Judaism started in the late 19th century. Followers agree with the practices of Reform Judaism, but are more moderate on certain religious issues. For example, they retain many Jewish traditions while recognizing the need for changes and adaptation to modern life. Although head coverings are required in the synagogue, men and women worship together and services are conducted in Hebrew and the native language of the worshipers.

Reconstructionists see Judaism as a civilization, with the synagogue functioning as the center for all aspects of Jewish community life. The Reconstructionist service is similar to that of Conservative Judaism: men and women worship together. Women may also become rabbis.

The stylish Heidal Yehuda
Synagogue in Tel Aviv.

THE SYNAGOGUE

The Jewish house of worship is the synagogue or temple. It is considered the house of God and His people, or a place of assembly for people in the presence of God.

Modern synagogues have an auditorium where worshipers gather; a pulpit, or *bimah* ("BEE-mah"), where an eternal light symbolizes that the light of the Torah will never be extinguished; and a Holy Ark, where the Scrolls of the Torah, the holiest scriptures, are kept.

Synagogues must have windows, for they are considered retreats for life rather than retreats from life. In traditional temples, there is a washbasin and pitcher in the lobby, so that worshipers can pour water over their hands as an act of cleansing. In addition, modern synagogues face eastward, toward Jerusalem.

THE TORAH AND THE TALMUD

"Torah" means "to teach" in Hebrew. The Torah is the first five books of the Old Testament. Also known as the Pentateuch, it is made up of the books of Genesis, Exodus, Leviticus, Numbers, and Deuteronomy, and contains the entire body of traditional religious teaching and study. Moses is credited with writing the Torah, having received the inspiration at Mount Sinai.

In the synagogue, the Torah is in the form of a parchment scroll and is considered sacred. It is covered by highly decorated, rich fabric.

The Talmud is a collection of 63 books of writings of ancient rabbis, and discussions of the classification of religious and civil law by generations of scholars. It is also concerned with every aspect of Jewish life, from ethics to diet, because Jewish religion and community are so closely related.

The study of the Talmud is central to Judaism. There are two versions of the Talmud: the Palestinian Talmud and the Babylonian Talmud.

Israeli Christians gather during Easter Sunday in Jerusalem.

CHRISTIANITY

The Christians of Israel represent all branches of Christendom and live mainly in Jerusalem, Bethlehem, Nazareth, Haifa, and Jaffa. Among the most common Christian communities in Israel are the Eastern Orthodox, Roman Catholic, Gregorian Armenian, Armenian Catholic, Syrian Catholic, Greek Melkite, Maronite, Syrian Orthodox, and Evangelical Christian.

As a rule, each community is headed by a patriarch who is assisted by an advisory council or an archbishop. Israel's Christian communities have their headquarters in Jerusalem, where the revered Church of the Holy Sepulcher is located. This house of worship is equally sacred to all Christian denominations, but it is mainly controlled by the Armenian, Greek Orthodox, and Roman Catholic churches.

The most ancient church group in the Holy Land is the Greek Orthodox, which emerged before the middle of the second century. It gained importance during the reign of Emperor Constantine.

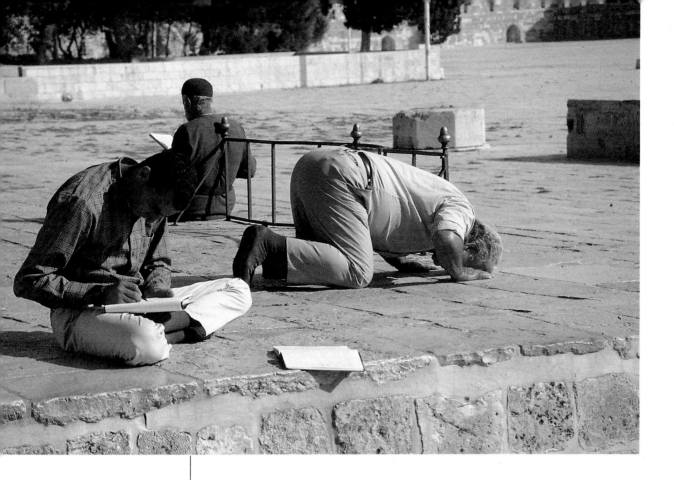

Muslims kneeling in prayer and studying the Koran.

ISLAM

Islam is the religion of Muslims, who make up the second largest religious group in Israel. According to Islamic belief, the angel Gabriel appeared to the prophet Mohammed in a vision, and told him to teach God's words to the world. Mohammed, who lived in the 6th century, preached that there is only one God, and that he (Mohammed) was the messenger of God. His companions recorded or memorized his revelations. These eventually became the holy writings of the Koran.

Muslims believe in only one God (whom they call Allah), that Mohammed is His prophet, and that there will be a judgment day. According to Islamic doctrine, the last prophet was Mohammed.

Muslims pray five times a day facing the holy city of Mecca in Saudi Arabia. Prayer time is announced by a crier, or *muezzin* ("moo-EH-zin"), from a tower in the mosque. The chief religious official is an *imam* ("im-AHM"), who leads people in prayer.

The mosque is the most important building for Muslims. The word mosque comes from the Arabic word *masjid* ("MAHS-jid," place of kneeling). Within the mosque, there is a *mihrab* ("MI-rahb," prayer niche) that points toward Mecca, a pulpit for the preacher, and a reading stand for the Koran. Most mosques have a minaret, a courtyard for washing before prayer, and a *madrasa* ("MAH-drah-sah") or school.

Drinking liquor, gambling, and eating pork are forbidden in Islam. During the holy month of Ramadan, adult Muslims must go without eating or drinking from sunrise to sunset. A pilgrimage to Mecca, the birthplace of Mohammed, is required in life. Charity is also a requirement; Muslims must give 2.5% of their wealth to the needy each year.

Like all religions, Islam has sects. Most Israeli Muslims belong to the Sunni sect. They believe that after Mohammed's death, leadership passed to the successors of Mohammed's tribe. The Shiites, the second largest sect, believe leadership passed on to descendants of Mohammed's son-in-law.

Islam is an Arabic word that means commitment or submission. Its followers are those who commit themselves in surrender to the will of Allah (God).

THE KORAN

The sacred scriptures of Islam were written in Arabic and the book of these scriptures is called the Koran. It contains 114 surahs ("SOO-rahs," chapters) that serve as a guide for life in the Islamic community. The book is a timeless source of guidance for Muslims, and it is studied wherever Islam exists.

The first official edition of the Koran appeared around A.D. 650, and a copy was sent to each mosque in the capital cities of the Muslim world. In some parts, the Koran resembles the Bible, early Christian writings not included in the New Testament, and the Talmud.

As an ancient sacred scripture, the Koran is highly symbolic. It therefore defies translation, for a single word can have many levels of significance. Meaning is limited to the interpretation by the translator.

DRUZE

The Druze derives their name from Mohammed al-Darazi, a founder of the sect. While this community speaks Arabic and their outward social and cultural patterns are not too different from other people's, they are distinguished by a strong sense of loyalty and unity. There is an effective ban on intermarriage and conversion of non-Druze to the sect that further separates this community from other Arabs. The Druze faction originated around 1000 B.C. but only gained official recognition in Israel in 1957.

The religion is called Din al-Tawhid by the Druze. Though Druze beliefs and rituals remain largely secret, it is known that the people believe in a god that operates through a system of five cosmic principles, and that there are periodic human appearances of the deity.

The Druze divide members of their faith into two groups: those who know the beliefs completely and those who do not. The first group consists of fewer than 10% of the total Druze population.

BAHA'I

The Baha'i faith was established in the mid-1800s in what is now Iraq. The efforts of Mirza Ali Mohammed, a 19th-century Persian mystic, are the inspiration behind this religion.

According to the Baha'is, a series of prophets were sent to teach moral truths and social principles. The last of these prophets was Baha'u'llah.

Baha'u'llah proclaimed the importance of all religions worshiping one God and that service to other human beings is the most significant act. He also said that God wants a united society based on mutual love and acceptance, and stressed moral and social improvement.

The international governing body of the faith, the Universal House of Justice, meets in Haifa.

One group of religious Israelis, the Samaritans, claim to be related to those Jews who were not deported by the Assyrians in 722 B.C. when the kingdom of Israel fell. In their religion, they observe only the first five books of the Old Testament, live in semi-isolation, marry only their own people, and pray in Hebrew. The phrase "good Samaritan" comes from the story Jesus told of them in the Bible.

THE DEAD SEA SCROLLS

One day in 1947, a young Bedouin shepherd who was innocently exploring a cave made one of the greatest archeological finds in history. In this cave in the cliffs overlooking the Dead Sea, he found a set of parchment and papyrus scrolls containing religious writings that had been preserved in earthenware jars for more than 2,000 years.

The recovered documents, now known as the Dead Sea Scrolls, were written by the ancient Hebrews who lived on what is now the site of Qumran. Thought to be members of the Essene sect, this devoutly religious group hid its sacred writings in the cave in anticipation of war with the Romans at around A.D. 66. The Essene community was destroyed, but its writings lived on, safely hidden for the ages.

After the initial discovery, archeological digs unearthed additional scrolls and fragments in 11 other caves. Years of study and careful reconstruction revealed the history of a community that removed itself from typical Jewish life, following a "teacher of righteousness" into the wilderness.

The scrolls tell much about the history of Jews, Christianity, and the Bible. Some were written in the sacred language of Hebrew, while others were written in Aramaic, which was the everyday tongue of the Palestinians of that time. Approximately one-fourth of the scrolls are biblical writings; each book of the Old Testament, except the book of Esther, is represented. A complete copy of the book of Isaiah was found, and it is believed to be the oldest copy.

The Dead Sea Scrolls are currently housed at the Shrine of the Book in Jerusalem, a museum devoted to these manuscripts. The scrolls have long been the subject of controversy, because Israeli authorities have restricted access to them to a very small group of international scholars.

However, in 1990, two scholars from the Hebrew Union College in Cincinnati published a volume of computer-generated reconstruction text of the scroll. This edition, made from photographic negatives of the scrolls that recently became available at the Huntington Library in California, was made available to all qualified scholars. Losing their monopoly on the texts, the Israeli Antiquities Authority subsequently agreed to allow access to the scrolls.

LANGUAGE

ISRAEL HAS TWO OFFICIAL LANGUAGES: Hebrew and Arabic. Hebrew is the mother tongue of approximately 60% of the population. Arabic is spoken by many older Oriental Jews, and Yiddish by older Ashkenazim and Ultraorthodox Jews.

Arabic is taught in Israel's Arab schools and used in legal affairs and in the legislature. French is also taught in most schools. English is a *lingua franca* in Israel, which means that it is used as a common or commercial language among people who do not speak the same language. In fact, money, postage stamps, and road signs are printed in English as well as in Hebrew and Arabic, and English is a compulsory subject in schools. Very few Israelis speak only one language.

Opposite: **An Orthodox Jew reading the Torah at the Wailing Wall.**

Left: **Even fast food has gone Hebrew! A Wendy's restaurant in Israel.**

HEBREW

Hebrew has long been the language of Judaism and, for many years, the Jews. It belongs to the Semitic-Hamitic family of languages and was used by the Hebrews when they took possession of Canaan around 1800 B.C. This language family is not only famous for giving Western civilization the language of the Old Testament, but also for the Phoenician alphabet, upon which our present alphabet is based.

The Hebrew language is divided into six developmental periods: pre-Biblical, Biblical, Dead Sea Scrolls, Mishnaic, Medieval, and Modern. Like any language, Hebrew has undergone changes throughout its history, but unlike most, there were not many changes until the Modern period. The main reason for this is that Hebrew was not spoken (except in prayer) from the time the Jews were driven from Roman Palestine in the 2nd century until the beginning of the 20th century.

Though the spoken language has changed by acquiring the thousands of words needed to become functional in the modern world, the written language has remained

Even farmers take time off from working the fields to read Hebrew.

quite unchanged. In fact, today's Israeli high school student can easily read and understand the original text of the Bible. The revival of Hebrew after 1,800 years of inactivity was due largely to the enormous work of Eliezer Ben-Yehuda, who emigrated to Palestine in 1881.

ELIEZER BEN-YEHUDA Ben-Yehuda was responsible for the relentless task of creating modern words from ancient Hebrew roots. But without the

THE HEBREW ALPHABET

The Hebrew alphabet consists of 22 letters, five of which have a different form when they appear at the end of a word. It is quite different from the English alphabet, for it has no capital letters or vowels.

In the 8th century, a system was developed for indicating vowels through the use of dots and dashes. These signs (called diacritics) are usually seen only in textbooks for students and children, making it very difficult for a reader who is unfamiliar with Hebrew to know how to pronounce a word. Only when a word is part of a sentence can the reader know the intended meaning. Hebrew, like most Semitic languages, is read from right to left.

Because Israelis come from so many different nations and cultures, the media must accommodate many language needs. Daily newspapers are printed in Arabic, English, French, Polish, Hungarian, German, and Yiddish.

cooperation of the Jews of Palestine, who eventually began to speak the language, Hebrew would have remained only a scriptural language.

Cooperation was slow in coming, however. At first, Orthodox rabbis denounced the attempt as dishonoring the scriptures, and Zionist leader Theodor Herzl felt that speaking the language was not practical. But because language is closely tied to a culture's identity, the Jews of the world who were returning to their homeland finally accepted that Hebrew would be a unifying force. What made the acceptance of Hebrew successful was that Ben-Yehuda transformed a complex language into one that is simple, logical, and modern. This allowed the millions of present and future immigrants to master the language easily and quickly.

Ben-Yehuda published a Hebrew newspaper and a 16-volume standard dictionary. In addition, he gathered a group of scholars to form a council, known today as the Hebrew Language Academy (Vaad Ha-Lashon— "vahd ah-lah-SHAWN"), to develop modern words. The academy continues to search the Bible and ancient Hebrew texts for words they can adapt to modern meanings. For example, for the word babysitter, they combined the words for "young child" and "guard."

When Ben-Yehuda started speaking Hebrew just over 100 years ago, it had a limited vocabulary of 7,500 words. Today, Hebrew consists of more than 100,000 words, largely because of the tireless efforts of the Vaad Ha-Lashon. Words borrowed from other languages have also greatly contributed to the Hebrew lexicon.

Road signs to the Dead Sea in Hebrew, Arabic, and English.

ARABIC

Arabic is the mother tongue of about 115 million Middle Eastern people, spoken in a broad belt from the Arabian Peninsula all the way to the Atlantic Ocean. It is the language of Islam and the Koran and, in 1974, was named the sixth official language of the United Nations.

As a Semitic language, Arabic is closely related to Hebrew. In fact, Hebrew borrows frequently from Arabic. While individual Arabic words are frequently used in Hebrew, when it comes to colorful proverbs or curses, Israelis borrow entire Arab phrases!

Spoken Arabic varies from country to country, but classical Arabic (the language of the Koran) has remained essentially unchanged since the 7th century. The alphabet is composed of 28 letters, which are basically consonants. Vowel signs, as in Hebrew, are indicated by marks above and below the letters. Typical of Semitic languages, Arabic is read from right to left.

YIDDISH

Yiddish, spoken by many older Ashkenazim Israelis until approximately 50 years ago, was the language of the Jews of Eastern and Central Europe. It is a German dialect that is written in Hebrew characters. Vowels, however, are written in Yiddish.

This language arose around the 9th century as Jews adapted German to their needs by adding Hebrew words that were a part of their religious life. As Jews migrated eastward, Yiddish picked up Slavic influences. It greatly reflects its culture: there are few terms descriptive of nature, which Eastern European Jews had little contact with, and it is loaded with descriptive terms of character and about relations between people. Yiddish continues to be spoken by Ultraorthodox Jews in Israel as they feel it is wrong to use Hebrew as an everyday language.

ISRAELI NAMES

A clear indication of how Hebrew has come to represent the Zionist spirit is evident in Israeli names. So eager were many Jews to become a part of their homeland that they took new Hebrew last names. Those who were able to translate their names into Hebrew did so.

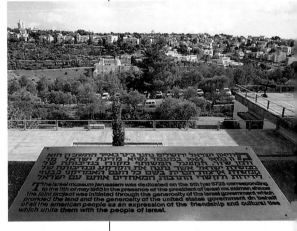

People named Schneider (German for "tailor") became Hayati; Weiss ("white" in German) was changed to Livni. Others chose last names representing their favorite regions, such as Galili (Galilee), Negbi (Negev), or Yerushalmi (Jerusalem).

A plaque in the Israel Museum in Jerusalem.

Many newcomers selected names symbolic of their self-image or after their parents or children. Avigad is a common Israeli last name that simply means "father of Gad." Eliezer Ben-Yehuda was Eliezer Perelman before emigrating to Palestine. Here, he preferred to be known as "son of Judea." Ami, Avi, Bat, or Ben at the beginning of last names mean "mother of," "father of," "daughter of," and "son of," respectively.

Others who took Hebrew surnames included prime ministers like David Ben-Gurion (previously David Green) and Golda Meir (Goldie Meyerson). Ben-Gurion felt so strongly about this that he made name-changing a requirement for public servants and government officials.

Biblical first names such as Benjamin, Naomi, Esther, David, and Ezra remain popular. However, many people are naming their children after beautiful Hebrew words. Names like Ayala (deer), Dafna (laurel), Orli (my light), Ari (lion), Eitan (strong, firm), and Gad (fortune) are popular.

ARTS

THE JEWISH PEOPLE have a long history of accomplishment in the arts. The first known work of Jewish literature is, of course, the Bible. Jewish art and architecture also date back to long ago. From the time Moses asked Bezalel to craft a gold menorah and an ark for the Ten Commandments, the Jewish people have made beautiful jewelry, pottery, and, on a larger scale, temples and castles.

From the time of the dispersal of the Jewish people in the second century, until 1948 when the state of Israel was established, Jewish art evolved and flourished, but it had no homeland. However, since almost a century ago, Jewish artists and their art have returned to the Holy Land.

Opposite: **An artist drawing in the Courtyard of the Prophets.**

Left: **Chalices, goblets, cooking pots, oil lamps, and baking trays found in the ruins of Tel Kadesh Barnea in the Negev Desert. The town was a frontier fort for the southern part of King Solomon's kingdom in the 10th century B.C.**

91

THE PERFORMING ARTS

Music has contributed greatly to the cultural advancement and international reputation of Israel. The Israel Philharmonic Orchestra, founded in 1936, has had many famous musicians and conductors among its ranks. Israelis are tremendously devoted to the Philharmonic; its 36,000 subscribers make it the most widely supported orchestra (per capita) in the world. It is said that residents of Tel Aviv read the obituaries in hopes of recognizing the name of someone they knew who happened to be a ticket holder!

Israel's music in the early years of statehood was very much in the folk tradition, with a biblical focus. It has since gone away from the religious and toward the political. Described as sad but optimistic, it touches on the things that are on the minds of the Israelis, such as peace, war, and even the Holocaust.

Jews have always loved music; folk, jazz, and pop music are popular in Israel. The many cultural groups that have come together have blended to create a musical form that is distinctly Israeli. One popular singer, Ofra Haza, has even recorded a 16th-century Yemenite prayer,

The Jerusalem Theater.

sung to rap music; it sold more than a million albums worldwide.

Israelis also love the theater. There are five major acting companies in the country, and Israelis lead the world in per capita theater attendance. Habima, the national theater company, has been producing plays since 1932. It performs three times daily, six days a week, to near capacity crowds. Beersheba, Jerusalem, and Haifa have repertory acting companies, and community theaters flourish throughout the land, including on the kibbutz.

LITERATURE

There is no continuous literary tradition in Hebrew because it was not spoken from the second century until the late 19th century. Hebrew appeared only in religious writing until a rebirth of Hebrew prose and poetry began in Russia and Eastern Europe in the 19th century.

The literature of Israel is made up of the works of two main groups of writers. The first group consists of authors who came to Israel in the First Aliyah. Their works reflect on the problems of adjusting to a new life in pre-independent Jerusalem. S.Y. Agnon, perhaps the best known writer of this group, won the 1966 Nobel Prize for Literature for his fictional works, cited for his "profoundly characteristic narrative art with motifs from the life of the Jewish people." Other writings from this literary group deal mainly with topics such as the Holocaust and the gathering and absorbing of Jews of various ethnic groups. Chaim Hazaz and Aaron Appelfeld are other well-known writers of this group.

The second group of Israeli authors is mainly made up of sabras whose works focus on the personality, problems, and struggle for existence of the young nation. The best-selling Israeli novel, *My Michael* by Amos Oz, is set against a background of war, as is the moving poetic work of Micha Bar-Am. The works of these two men have been translated into many languages and are widely read in Israel and throughout the world. A.B. Yehoshua and David Grossman are two other well-known Israeli authors who represent this second literary group.

Israelis are avid readers of foreign works as well. Because translating world-famous classics and modern literature into Hebrew is an ongoing process, the availability of world literature in Israel's official language is greeted with great enthusiasm. UNESCO statistics rank Israel No. 2 in terms of book readership.

Israeli literature for children has improved tremendously in recent years. Every year, several hundred children's books are published. Youth sections of public libraries and book stores have expanded and are always filled with eager readers or buyers. The style of writing for children's literature reflects a world trend toward a more direct approach to language and content.

A young girl riding her bicycle under an artist's modern work at the Tel Aviv Museum.

VISUAL ARTS

Israelis are fond of art, and an original artwork can usually be found in even the smallest apartment. There are countless art galleries in the cities—especially Tel Aviv—and for a country of its size, Israel has many museums. These museums are found in cities and even on the kibbutz, housing treasures of archeology and local history, ancient and modern artworks, and primitive and sophisticated craftworks.

An attempt at an Israeli style in painting was started by the Bezalel School of Arts and Craft, which was founded in Jerusalem in 1906. The style combined traditional Jewish themes and images with modern Western concepts, but over the years, newness and originality have been the major element in Israeli art. The result is that there is no single identifiable Israeli "school" of art.

ISRAEL'S FIRST ART SCHOOL

The Bezalel School of Arts and Crafts in Jerusalem was founded by sculptor Boris Schatz. His aim was to foster some form of connection between the Jewish people and "handwork." Schatz's goal was not to promote and present the art of the Israelis, but to encourage the creation of original art.

The Bezalel School struggled financially in its early years, and in 1928, lost the struggle. It remained shut until 1935 when painter Joseph Budko, along with European artists and teachers who emigrated to Israel, re-opened the school.

The school has offered programs in all arts and craft areas, and Israel's most respected artists have attended the institution. Teachers from all over the world are among the faculty at the school, which in the late 1960s attained the status of Academy of Arts and Design. It is now considered the supreme arts institution in Israel.

There have been a few art movements in Israel. "New Horizons" in the 1950s dedicated itself to the advancement of abstract tendencies. "102" was established sometime later, but the artists of these movements remained true to their individuality.

In recent years, Israeli artwork has been exhibited at the Jewish Museum in New York. The show, called *Artists of Israel. 1920–1980*, included pieces by well-known artists like Reuven Rubin, Tziona Tagger, Yosef Zaritsky, and Yaakov Agam.

A younger generation of work was also represented, and the number of successful women artists shows that there is equal opportunity in the arts in Israel. Artist communities, run on a cooperative basis, are located near Haifa and in Old Jaffa.

THE INBAL DANCE THEATER

Traditions of the Yemenite Jews, who came to Israel in great numbers after the establishment of the state of Israel, have been celebrated by the Inbal Dance Theater since it was founded in Israel in 1949. It was started by Sara Levi-Tenai, who wanted to preserve the artistic heritage of the Yemenite Jews.

The Yemenites were isolated from mainstream Judaism for 2,000 years; the music and dance forms they brought to their new home are reminders of ancient religious rituals and ceremonies.

Yemenite music and story-telling accompany the traditional dance movements, which include rhythmic walking, exciting head and body movements, and captivating hand gestures.

Inspiration for Inbal dances comes not only from Yemenite traditions, but also Israeli shepherd and southern coastal Arabian dances. The themes of the company's dances are based on the Bible and religious customs.

Dancers performing in front of the Jerusalem Theater during the Jerusalem Festival.

DANCE

Dance has always been an integral part of Jewish life. There are many biblical references to it as an expression of joy and religious excitement, and the Jews have incorporated dance into many types of ceremonies.

In Israel, dance remains important. The various ethnic groups that have emigrated to the Holy Land brought many dance forms, among them the *debka* ("DAB-kah"), which is an Arabic line dance performed by men, and the *hora* ("HORE-uh"), an Eastern European circle dance. Among Ultraorthodox Jews, there is strict separation of the sexes in dance, so participants hold the ends of a handkerchief to prevent physical contact.

Community folk dancing is a part of modern Israeli culture. After the Sabbath on Saturday evenings, Israelis join in folk dancing in local parks and on the kibbutzim.

Professional dance groups are heavily supported in Israel. There are three major modern dance institutions, professional folk-dance groups, and even a hearing-impaired dancers' troupe.

ARCHITECTURE

In Israel, all styles of architecture combine, from the traditional Arab-style villas that blend into the surrounding landscape, and the simple tile-roofed houses of the first settlers, to the modern European forms of seaside cottages.

After the post-World War I and World War II mass immigrations, the *shikkun* ("shi-KOON," housing project) became necessary to accommodate the increase in population, with an emphasis on usefulness rather than beauty. Nonetheless, since statehood, Israeli architects have attempted to introduce style and grace into new institutions. Higher education campuses led the way in the creation of structures with a style that could be characterized as Israeli; the Hebrew University Givat Ram campus in Jerusalem, the Technion in Haifa, and the Weizmann Institute in Rehovot are all examples of beautifully designed, highly functional buildings.

Other public buildings with notable architecture are the Israel Museum Complex in Jerusalem, the Knesset, concert halls, and the Jerusalem and Haifa theaters.

LEISURE

THE LEISURE ACTIVITIES OF THE ISRAELI PEOPLE are influenced by a few very important factors. First of all, there is little leisure time. Israelis work (and go to school) six days a week. Their one day off is the Sabbath when few, if any, businesses are open and public transportation does not run. Added to this is the fact that the typical Israeli has little money for recreation after all the bills are paid.

Having said that, the most popular leisure activity in Israel is visiting. On weekday evenings, people visit friends and family. Adults get together quite often for coffee and cake. On Friday evenings, even the least religious of families have their version of the traditional Sabbath dinner, which usually includes lighting candles.

Opposite: **Riding the rapids at the Jordan River.**

Left: **Israelis and their model airplanes.**

Vacationers at the beach in Tel Aviv.

IN PURSUIT OF LEISURE

There is a strong emphasis on physical fitness in Israel, caused in part by the ever-ready nature of the Israeli Defense Forces. So, sports and outdoor or nature activities such as hiking hold much interest.

Much of the Israelis' free time is spent outdoors. People love to go out to eat; food vendors are everywhere, offering a variety of international fast foods from the Middle Eastern *falafel* ("fuh-LAH-fehl," spicy ground chickpea balls) to New York-style hot dogs. Outdoor cafés are very popular. While enjoying a cup of iced coffee, many people get together to play chess and backgammon, or argue about politics and world affairs.

As in any country, some of the types of leisure activities that the inhabitants enjoy are determined by locality. The health clubs, swimming pools, and chic shopping districts of Tel Aviv are not convenient for the residents of any other city or town because they are too far away.

Some interests that are shared by all Israelis are reading, going to the movies, watching television, listening to the radio, and attending concerts and the ballet.

SPORTS

Sports have become increasingly important in Israel in recent years. There are many sports clubs, as well as facilities and equipment, provided to the population by both the government and private organizations.

Soccer is by far Israel's favorite sport; all activity seems to stop on the afternoon of an important soccer match. Spectators tend to become quite involved in the game, especially if they do not agree with an important decision by the referee. Israel has a soccer team that competes internationally, and a national league in which teams compete against one another on a regular basis.

Basketball is growing in popularity. One Israeli team, Maccabi Tel Aviv, has twice captured the European Cup championship. There is also a 12-team professional league with many American-born players.

Interest in tennis is growing by leaps and bounds. The country's climate is perfect for outdoor participation throughout the year, and as a result there are tennis courts or stadiums in most cities and towns. Two Israeli professional tennis players, Shlomo Glickstein and Amos Mansdorf, have been ranked among the top competitors in the world.

Hiking is a great national passion. On Saturday afternoons, countless families pack into their cars and set out for national parks for a picnic and to explore the country on foot. An organized annual springtime hiking event that is a three-day march through the hills of Judea and Samaria has attracted participants ranging from teenagers to people in their 70s. Those who finish the march parade victoriously through Jerusalem.

Desert hikers stop by a pool for a rest.

THE MACCABIAH GAMES

In 1993, Israel again hosted the Maccabiah Games, an Olympics-style sporting event for Jewish athletes from around the world. The goal of the games is to bring Jews together in the Holy Land and to promote physical excellence and well-being.

Joseph Yekutieli founded the Maccabiah Games in 1932. In the first games, approximately 500 athletes from 23 countries participated, and many later remained in Palestine to become citizens. For the second Maccabiah Games in 1935, nearly 2,000 athletes came. However, the third games did not take place until 1950, first postponed because of World War II, and later due to the establishment of the state of Israel.

Today, the Maccabiah Games are held in Tel Aviv every four years. Events include table tennis, basketball, volleyball, track and field, tennis, boxing, soccer, swimming, water polo, gymnastics, fencing, and wrestling.

Like the Olympics, the Maccabiah Games have dramatic and moving opening and closing ceremonies, which are attended by top Israeli officials.

TELEVISION

Israelis love to watch television, not just for the sake of entertainment; newscasts provide important information for a country where war can start at any time. The length of the newscast depends on the amount of news, but on an average day, it runs for 30 minutes. Apart from the news, Israelis enjoy the same type of television entertainment as do North Americans. In fact, much of Israeli television fare is imported from the United States.

Israeli TV is mainly broadcast on one channel. From morning until about 5 p.m., educational programs are aired, including *Rehov Sum-Sum* ("ray-HOVE sum-sum"), the Hebrew version of *Sesame Street*, and cartoons. Perhaps the reason they are called "educational" is because children have to read Hebrew subtitles!

Arabic television follows the educational broadcasts. For three hours, the Israeli Arab minority, residents of the occupied territories, and any Arab in the neighboring countries who is interested, tune in to the Arabic news (reputed to be the most reliable) and other Arabic-language programs. Israelis can also watch Jordanian and Syrian television, because the Middle Eastern electronic media have no national boundaries.

American programs are very popular and are aired after the Arabic programs. Israeli TV also imports programs from Europe, Canada, and Australia. There are no commercials on Israeli TV.

Another television station, known as "The Second Channel," was recently started, but its broadcasts are limited and, in some areas, a special antenna is required to receive it. American news programs like *Nightline, The McNeil-Lehrer Report*, and *Cable News Network* are carried on this station.

Cable television has become available to Israelis, putting them in touch with TV stations all over the world. Video tapes are also popular. In cities and towns throughout the country, no matter how small or religious, there are video stores with large selections of movies.

RADIO

Radio is also an Israeli passion. Bus drivers turn up the volume of the hourly newscasts so that passengers can hear all the latest news; and during times of great crisis, Israelis are never without radios by their side.

Israel has a major news station that employs the finest journalists who are constantly interviewing top Israeli officials, including the prime minister, and giving reports and commentary on economic and international news. There is also a military radio station that not only presents four newscasts daily, but also jazz and rock music.

The Israeli Broadcasting Authority broadcasts programs for local and overseas listeners in 16 languages, including Hebrew, Arabic, English, French, Russian, and Spanish. It gears its programming to the needs of Israel's immigrants. The musical tastes of the young and old are also satisfied. One station beats out rock tunes all day long and into the night, while another dedicated to classical music soothes thousands with its 18 hours of broadcasting each day.

One of the balloons in the International Hot Air Balloon Competition at Arad near the Dead Sea.

FESTIVALS

THE WORD "FESTIVAL" brings to mind a wild celebration that commemorates notable events. Often, however, there is a serious reason behind the festivities, and some of the rituals and traditional activities are actually somber in tone.

In Israel, holy land to three of the world's great religions, there is a full range of celebrations—from religious and secular to solemn and cheerful.

THE LUNAR CALENDAR

Holidays in Israel are set according to the lunar calendar (the calendar of the Bible), so each year holidays fall on a different day than they did the year before. Israelis live their daily lives by the calendar that starts with January and ends with December (the Gregorian calendar), but observe their holidays according to one that starts with Tishre and ends with Elul. If the date is July 8, 1992 on the Gregorian calendar, it is Tammuz 7, 5752 on the Hebrew calendar. If you don't believe it, just check the top of *The Jerusalem Post*; it gives the Gregorian, Hebrew, and Muslim dates. (According to the Muslim calendar, the year 1995 is 1415.)

The 12 Hebrew months begin with the appearance of the new moon, and each month has 29 or 30 days. To prevent the lunar year from slipping too far behind the solar year (upon which the Gregorian calendar is based), every few years an extra month, called Adar Bet, is added.

The Muslim calendar also has 12 months that begin with the new moon. However, it does not make an attempt to relate the lengths of the solar and lunar years, and a holiday that occurs in the summer one year can fall in the winter a few years later.

Following a lunar year schedule can have some very interesting results. For example, when the state of Israel celebrates the day of independence, which was on May 14, 1948, it celebrates the occasion on the fifth day of the month of Iyyar, which will not fall on May 14 again until the year 2005.

Opposite: **All dressed up and ready to go! Teens wear their costumes to celebrate Purim (Feast of Esther).**

JEWISH HOLIDAYS

Since ancient times, Jews have cherished and observed their holy days. The rituals were a uniting force for the Jews of the Diaspora, and the holidays themselves served as reminders of their strong leadership and exceptional circumstances. Some of the holidays celebrated in Israel originated more than 3,000 years ago. Over the years, when the Jews met great challenges, they added more memorable days to their festivals calendar.

ROSH HASHANAH

The High Holy Days (Rosh Hashanah and Yom Kippur) mark the beginning of the Jewish year. According to tradition, God opens three books on Rosh Hashanah—one for the wicked, one for the righteous, and one for all others. The names of the righteous are written in the Book of Life; the wicked are designated for death in the coming year; and judgment on the rest is suspended for a 10-day period of personal accounting and atonement that occurs between Rosh Hashanah and Yom Kippur. A

One highlight of Rosh Hashanah is when the ram's horn, or *shofar* ("show-fahr"), is trumpeted. For Jews everywhere, the *shofar* is a memorable symbol of the Jewish New Year. For Israelis, it represents not only the start of the holiday, but an alarm in times of war.

typical greeting among Jews during this holiday season is, "May you be inscribed in the Book of Life."

Rosh Hashanah falls in September or October. While the holiday has a serious overtone, the new year is welcomed with a sense of joy. After attending synagogue services, Jewish families gather for a festive meal. Jewish delicacies are prepared as omens of good luck. The following night, new fruits are eaten for the first time and a special blessing is recited. This holiday is extremely popular because it is the only one in the entire year that is observed for two consecutive days. Israelis take advantage of the break by making trips to the beach, organizing picnics and barbecues, or hiking in the country's national parks.

YOM KIPPUR

On Yom Kippur, Jews make their peace with God and their conscience. It is said that the names merely written in God's books on Rosh Hashanah are sealed on Yom Kippur, judgment having been made after an appropriate period of soul-searching and asking for forgiveness from God.

Yom Kippur has been observed since the days of Moses. On this solemn day, Jews refrain from eating and drinking to atone for the sins of the past year. Their fast begins at sundown on the eve of Yom Kippur and ends at sundown on Yom Kippur with a large meal shared by the whole family.

SUKKOT AND SIMCHAT TORAH

Shortly after the High Holy Days, traditional Jews celebrate Sukkot (Harvest Festival) over a period of eight days. Families build a *sukkah* ("SOO-kuh," hut) next to their homes, representing the dwelling of the ancient Jews who wandered the desert after their escape from Egypt.

Sukkot is the most visible festival in Israel. Even secular kibbutzniks build the *sukkah*. In their case, however, the *sukkah* symbolizes the Diaspora. Israelis who celebrate the religious aspect of Sukkot eat their meals in the *sukkah* in thanksgiving at the close of the harvest season.

Simchat Torah (Rejoicing of the Law) falls on the last day of Sukkot and is celebrated with dancing, singing, and worship. It coincides with the completion of the reading of the Torah for the year. In the synagogue, a parade precedes a ceremonial unrolling of a Torah scroll to the first chapter, and the reading of the first five books of the Bible begins anew.

All of Israel comes to a virtual standstill on Yom Kippur; public transportation does not run, television and radio stations do not broadcast, and there are no cars on the most traveled roads. Even secular Jews, who normally avoid the ritual part of everyday Jewish life, observe this traditional day of rest, physical sacrifice, and deep thought.

HANUKKAH

Hanukkah is an eight-day festival that celebrates the victory of Judas Maccabee's warriors over the Syrians in the second century B.C. Upon victory, the Jews set out to rededicate the temple in Jerusalem, only to find that there was just enough oil to burn for one day. However, the oil miraculously burned for eight days. This is why candles are lit for the eight days of Hanukkah.

Hanukkah is enjoyed widely in Israel; families gather to party and eat traditional Hanukkah foods, and children receive gifts from their parents on each of the eight nights. In the village of Modin, where the Maccabees came from, a special relay race commemorates the holiday. The first runner lights the torch of freedom and independence and carries it to the next runner. The passing of the torch goes on until the last runner reaches Jerusalem and hands the torch to the president of Israel.

Perhaps because Israel is still fighting to maintain its freedom and because Hanukkah is a historical rather than a religious event, this is one holiday religious and secular Israelis alike have made their own.

A family lighting candles to celebrate Hanukkah.

PESACH

Pesach ("PAY-sock") or Passover, a springtime holiday, is a memorial of the Israelites' escape from hundreds of years of slavery in Egypt.

The word "passover" comes from the time when God sent an angel to slay the firstborn child of every Egyptian home, but "passed over" Jewish homes that were marked with blood from sacrificial lambs. The Egyptians

were so overcome by the tragedy that the Jews were able to escape. The opportunity to flee afforded the Jews no time to wait for the bread they were baking to rise, thus a restriction against bread with yeast is observed throughout Passover.

An important night is the evening of the Seder, which is a ceremonial dinner on the first night of this seven-day festival. The Seder recreates the events of the escape (or "exodus") from Egypt. A special storyline of the exodus called the *Hagadda* ("HOG-uh-dah") is read aloud. Celebrants (especially children) are asked to participate in answering questions from the *Hagadda* and eating the symbolic foods for the ceremony.

This holiday is also celebrated by both religious and the secular Jews, as it is a festival of freedom. Among secular Jews, the version of the storyline is sometimes altered so there is little mention of biblical characters. Nonetheless, Pesach remains a holiday that has an effect on all Israelis, if for no other reason than that it becomes impossible to buy bread during Passover week; all bakeries are closed except those in Arab villages.

MEMORIAL AND INDEPENDENCE

Independence Day has been celebrated only since 1948, when the state of Israel came into existence. The celebrations, on the fifth day of the Hebrew month of Iyyar, are preceded by Memorial Day, when Israelis remember those who gave their lives for the state.

During Memorial Day, television and radio stations broadcast documentaries on Israeli battles and their heroes. During the two-minute silence, work stops while cars and buses wait at the side of the road. At sundown, sirens scream across the country and the Independence Day celebrations begin. Families build bonfires on the hillsides and people sit around the fires to sing and tell stories. The next day, there are fireworks, parades, dancing in the streets, military air shows, concerts, and the International Bible Contest, which draws young people from all over the world. A song festival featuring the entertainment stars of the day is broadcast live.

CHRISTIAN HOLIDAYS

Followers of the Greek Orthodox and Armenian Orthodox churches gather to light candles in the Church of the Holy Sepulcher during Easter.

Like Christians everywhere, Israeli Christians celebrate Christmas, Good Friday, and Easter. During these holidays, church bells in the old section of Jerusalem ring, summoning Christians to walk where Jesus walked. Special services are held in churches.

At Christmas, Pilgrims gather around Manger Square in Bethlehem while beautiful music pours out of the Church of the Nativity. Christians also look out for Baba Noel, as Santa Claus is known in Israel, and decorate their houses with Christmas trees.

CALENDAR OF FESTIVALS

(Season of holidays in 1994)

AUTUMN
(Jewish) Rosh Hashanah (New Year)
(Jewish) Yom Kippur (Day of Atonement)
(Jewish) Sukkot (Harvest Festival)
(Jewish) Simchat Torah (Rejoicing of the
   Law)

WINTER
(Jewish) Hanukkah (Festival of Lights)
(Jewish) Tu B'Shvat (New Year of the
   Trees)
(Christian) Christmas

SPRING
(Islamic) Id-al-Fitr (Feast of Breaking the Fast)
(Jewish) Pesach (Passover)
(Christian) Good Friday
(Christian) Easter
(Jewish) Holocaust Memorial Day
(Jewish) Purim (Feast of Esther)
(Jewish) Memorial Day and Independence Day
(Islamic) Id-al-Adha (Feast of the Sacrifice)

SUMMER
(Jewish) Shavuot
(Islamic) Mawlid El-Nabi (Prophet Mohammed's
   Birthday)

Easter offers the most dramatic sight in Jerusalem, where hundreds of pilgrims make their way down the Via Dolorosa during Holy Week. This is the route Jesus took to Calvary, where he was crucified.

ISLAMIC HOLIDAYS

The most joyous of Muslim holidays occurs at the end of the fasting month of Ramadan, when there is a three-day feast called Id-al-Fitr. It is also a time for family visits. Sweet pastries are served and children receive gifts like clothing. People also dye their hands an orange-red with a natural dye called henna as a symbol of good luck.

Id-al-Adha, Feast of the Sacrifice, is also referred to as the "big holiday." It honors Abraham, the first man to believe in one God, and his son Ishmael. According to the Koran, God commanded Abraham to sacrifice his son, and because of his great love for God, Abraham obeyed. God saved Ishmael by substituting a lamb in his place. Muslims believe that Ishmael thus became the father of the Arab people, and they honor Ishmael by sacrificing a sheep on Id-al-Adha. Muslims also celebrate this holiday with sweet pastries, henna, and gifts. They roast a sheep and eat the meat in special festival dishes, giving any extra food to the poor.

Most Christians celebrate Christmas on December 25, but the Greek and Eastern Orthodox Christians in Israel celebrate it on January 6 and 7, while the Armenian Christians celebrate it on January 18 and 19.

FOOD

ISRAEL MAY BE A YOUNG NATION, but not so in its cuisine. People from all over the world have settled in the country, bringing with them regional and personal favorites that are perhaps centuries old. And in a very short time, Israel has developed its own genuine style of food.

Back in the 1940s, it was not clear whether a special Israeli cuisine would develop. Many thought that food was not important; there were more urgent matters to think about. Food was considered merely a source of energy. In addition, the women of Israel did not want to follow in the traditional footsteps of women in Eastern Europe, where the kitchen was the center of their lives. Now, however, Israelis enjoy preparing food, including traditional meals with an ethnic flair.

Opposite: **An Arab food market at the Damascus Gate in Jerusalem.**

Left: **The Tel Aviv Ha-Karmel market.**

ISRAELI FOODS

It is absolutely safe
to drink water
direct from the tap
in Israel. All the
country's drinking
water comes from
only one source—
the world's most
famous lake, the
Sea of Galilee.

The foods eaten in Israel today are a blend of many cultures. Native Israeli cuisine would be described as similar to that of the Arab nations, but the Oriental and European influence on the Israeli diet is unmistakable. A common thread in the exotic recipes that have come together in Israel is the religious and cultural traditions shared by the Jews of the world.

The Israeli food tradition was formed according to the availability (or lack) of certain foods. For example, fruits and vegetables, which are inexpensive and grown in large amounts, are included in virtually every meal. Dairy products, including different types of yogurt and soured milks and creams, are also a major part of the Israeli diet. Red meat is rarely eaten, partly because the lack of quality grazing land for livestock produces a lower grade of meat. Turkey and chicken are a major part of the Israeli diet.

The Jewish state's contribution to world cuisine is undoubtedly the Israeli breakfast. This outstanding meal has its roots in the kibbutz. In the early morning hours, kibbutz farmers have a light snack consisting of tea with toast and jam so that they can get to the fields before the day gets hot. It is after putting in a few hours of hard work that they return for breakfast.

A typical Israeli breakfast (especially on the kibbutz) consists of a delicious spread of vegetables (tomatoes, onions, green peppers, and radishes); olives; eggs; carrot salad; a wide variety of dairy products, including buttermilk, yogurt, cottage cheese, and hard cheeses; toast and breads; herring; hot cereals; coffee or tea. It is served buffet style and satisfies every individual's appetite.

For other meals, *falafel* sandwiches are favorites. Typically Middle Eastern, *falafel* sandwiches are filled with fried balls of chickpeas mixed with garlic, onion, and spices. They are usually served in pita bread with tahini sauce (sesame seed paste) poured over the *falafel*.

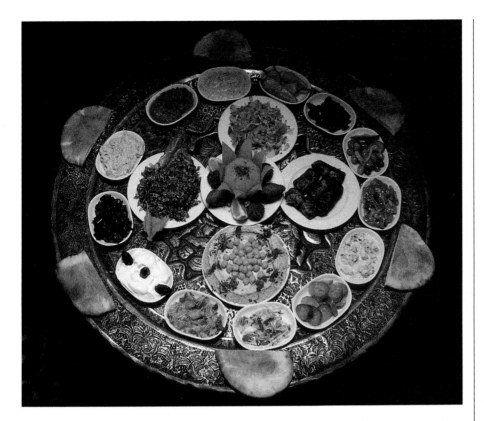

Another dish enjoyed throughout Israel is humus ("KOO-moos"), a smooth paste of chickpeas with garlic and tahini sauce. Other Arabic foods that are quite popular among the people of Israel are *shawarma* ("SHAH-wahr-mah," a spicy lamb usually served on pita), a marinated lamb dish called shashlik cooked on skewers over a flame, and shish kebab.

Cholent ("CHOE-luhn") is a stew traditionally served on the Jewish Sabbath, which is observed on Saturday. Because the oven in a religious home cannot be lit after sundown on Friday, *cholent* is a perfect meal; it simmers overnight in a warm oven turned on before the Sabbath. Various types of *cholent* reflect the traditional foods of the different Jewish ethnic groups. Moroccan Jews, for example, use beef, spices, chickpeas, and potatoes, while Sephardic Jews include beans, meat, potatoes, and eggs.

Kugel ("KOO-gehl"), a noodle casserole that is a traditional food among Eastern European Jews, is also a Sabbath favorite because it too can be left overnight in a warm oven and be ready for the meal on Saturday.

A fruit and vegetable vendor at the Tel Aviv Ha-Karmel market.

JEWISH DIETARY LAWS

Another factor that plays a significant role in the Israeli menu is the dietary laws of the Jews and Muslims.

Kashrut is the kosher dietary system for Jews. Foods that are permitted are referred to as kosher, which means "fit" or "proper." Those that are not are called *trefa* ("treh-FAH"). The dietary laws, which Jews have followed for thousands of years, are stated in the Bible and discussed extensively in the Talmud. Orthodox Jews believe that these laws are given by God and cannot be violated.

The *kashrut* falls into three categories: foods that can and cannot be eaten, the slaughter and preparation of meat, and the ways foods are served. (Since all *kashrut* rules involve animals, the Jewish vegetarian has little to worry about!)

The laws state that any animal with cloven (split) hoofs and that chews cud is edible; both criteria must be met. Therefore, lamb and beef are allowed; rabbit, camel, and pork are not. Birds that seize food in their claws (wild birds and birds of prey) are unclean and therefore prohibited. Buzzards, cranes, eagles, and owls are not acceptable; but turkey, chicken, duck, quail, and pigeon are allowed. Fish that have fins and scales are clean and can be consumed; those without, like catfish, porpoise, or shellfish like shrimp and lobster, are forbidden.

Animals, fish, and fowl that can be eaten must be slaughtered and prepared according to strict rules that include removing veins and arteries from the carcass. The meat must then be soaked in water and salted.

Rules for serving food state that dairy products and meat must not be eaten together. This separation is maintained throughout preparation, cooking, and eating, and separate sets of dishes, cookware, and silverware are required.

ISLAMIC DIETARY LAWS

Muslims also have dietary laws that are spelled out in the Koran. Foods that are permitted are referred to as *halal* ("hah-LULL"). These laws are also about eating and slaughtering animals, and though they differ from *kashrut*, they share some similarities. For example, consumption of blood and pork is prohibited.

Food that is found dead or has been offered to idols is not edible for the Muslim and, as is the case with Jews, animals must be slaughtered according to a ritual. Islamic laws say that during the slaughter, the butcher must call out the name of Allah. Muslims are also prohibited from drinking alcohol. They remain free of sin, however, if they are forced to consume prohibited food or drink.

HOLIDAY FOODS

All areas of Israeli life are influenced by the festivals and holy days of the Jewish year. So, too, are the foods eaten, because the festivals marking the holidays are usually observed by eating certain foods.

Bread galore! A man on his way to buy bread at the local Old City bakery in Jerusalem.

ROSH HASHANAH The Jewish year begins in autumn with Rosh Hashanah. Traditionally, sweet foods such as apples and honey are eaten to remind Jews of the sweetness of God's blessings. A round loaf of bread, called challah ("CHAH-lah"), is also consumed. The round bread reminds Jews that they are bound to the wheel of fate. People eat pieces dipped in honey to ensure a sweet year. Salads and sour foods are avoided; nothing should alter the sweetness of the beginning of the year.

YOM KIPPUR takes place 10 days after Rosh Hashanah. To atone for the sins of the past year, no food is eaten from the hour before sunset on the eve of Yom Kippur until after sunset the next day. Bland chicken and rice is eaten before the fast to help prevent thirst and indigestion. Then a morsel of bread and water is taken as a symbolic gesture of nourishment. After the fast, families and friends eat together, starting with apple dipped in honey. Herring or other salty food follows. The rest of the meal consists of traditional foods of particular ethnic groups.

SUKKOT This eight-day harvest festival is marked by Orthodox Jews eating meals in the *sukkah*, a hut decorated with fruits. Harvest foods such as figs, apricots, pomegranates, onions, barley, and lettuce are part of each meal. According to Jewish folklore, a woman will have a child after eating a lemon from the *sukkah* after Sukkot.

HANUKKAH The Festival of Lights is celebrated for eight days in the winter. It marks the time when a small amount of oil miraculously continued to burn in the rededicated temple in Jerusalem for eight days. Foods fried in oil, such as *latkes* ("LAHT-kees," potato pancakes) and *sufganiyot* ("soof-gah-ni-YOAT," doughnuts), are enjoyed during this holiday.

PURIM Also known as the Feast of Esther, this springtime festival celebrates the story of Queen Esther saving the Jewish people from a murderous tyrant, Haman. People eat Haman's Ears (*hamentashen*—"oo-

Israeli date palms.

muhn-TASH"), which are sweet cakes filled with prunes or poppy seeds. Wine is served, because Haman's defeat was due to the excessive amount of wine Esther served him. Traditional foods include chickpeas, *kreplach* ("KREH-plah," dumplings), and turkey.

PESACH or Passover celebrates the Jews' escape from Egypt. The fleeing Jews baked unleavened bread because they could not wait for the dough to rise. As a result, matzo (an unleavened cracker-like bread) is eaten. The first evening is marked by a ritual meal called a Seder, and for the remainder of the week, nothing leavened by yeast may be eaten. During the Seder, a special plate is prepared with foods recalling the trials of the Jews: for example, bitter herbs to remember the bitterness of Egyptian slavery.

A Tel Aviv Ashkenazim family celebrating a Passover meal.

SHAVUOT This eight-day holiday is the last festival of the year. It celebrates Moses receiving the Ten Commandments and the summer fruits coming into season. Dairy dishes such as cheese blintzes (pancakes) are served because Jews believe that when the Israelites returned from receiving the laws, the milk at their camp had turned sour (the first step in making cheese). Accompanying the milk products are honey biscuits to celebrate Israel being "the land of milk and honey."

SABBATH takes place on the seventh day of every week, starting at sundown Friday and ending at sundown Saturday. It is a special day of rest and prayer. Like all Jewish celebrations, the Sabbath (or Shabat) has its special foods, the most common being the challah, or Sabbath bread. Each family has its own special dishes that are enjoyed on Sabbath.

On the Sabbath, Orthodox Jews eat foods that do not require cooking on the day that they are eaten. For example, they eat gefilte fish (poached fishballs that are served cold) because it can be prepared in advance.

119

STREET FOODS

Israelis are always on the move, and because there is not much leisure time, people like to eat and run. Israel not only has a lively street vendor industry, it also has a booming gas station/fast-food trade. What started out as a convenience—filling up the gas tank and stomach at the same time—has turned popular. People dodge traffic to run and grab some *mezze* ("MEH-zee," a variety of appetizer), grilled meat or fish, and sweet Turkish coffee. People eat quickly and keep the traffic flowing.

For pedestrians, *falafel* is found almost everywhere. In fact, after paying for the first *falafel* on pita (a thin, flat bread), Israelis can have additional servings of the chickpea mixture while only paying for the pita.

Another tasty street food is *brik*, which is filo dough filled with cheese or potato. Bagels are sold warm on street corners, and some vendors offer a tasty dip called

A vendor recommending melons to a customer at the Mahaneh Yehuda Food Market.

za'atar ("ZAH-ah-tahr"). On the sweet side, a caramel-like custard called *malabi* ("MAH-lah-bee") is eaten from little tin cups. *Tamarindi* ("TAH-mah-reen-dee") is a favorite syrupy juice that street vendors carry in large jars on their shoulders. For fast food, hamburgers are available at MacDavid's, Israel's answer to McDonald's, and Burger Ranch. The similarities end there, however, because the hamburgers and hot dogs served in Israel are much spicier than those in the United States.

Perhaps the most common outdoor food is sunflower seeds; Israelis always seem to be eating them. The experienced seed eater can remove the meat and spit out the shell without ever taking a hand to the mouth. Discarded shells line the sidewalks and roadways, making sunflower seeds the ultimate street food in Israel!

RECIPE: KASHA CHOLENT

This Sabbath dish, prepared in advance on days when cooking is prohibited, is a hot meal-in-one for four to six people.

2 pounds beef brisket
1 large onion, diced finely
1 cup navy beans or kidney beans
1 cup coarse-milled buckwheat groats
1 cup grated raw carrot (optional)

$^1/_4$ teaspoon paprika (optional)
$^1/_2$ teaspoon salt
dash of pepper
4 cups boiling water

Sear the meat in a heavy pot with a tight-fitting lid. Add onion and stir until lightly browned. Add the other ingredients in the order listed, then cover and cook over moderate heat for $1^1/_2$ hours. Lift the lid to check that no additional water is needed, then put the pot on a warming tray so that the dish is kept simmering very gently. The traditional cholent dish is slow-cooked overnight and the following day till noon. Slice the beef and serve the dish while hot.

FOOD SHOPPING

Although the supermarket concept is the same as in the United States, a quick glance at the shelves reveals that the goods on display are a little different from what is sold in North America. Milk, for example, comes in clear plastic sacks; dishwashing liquid is actually a yellow paste in a pail. Items that are available in the United States in many different brands and flavors, like salad dressing, are quite limited in Israel.

But some Israelis never even go to the supermarket. In nearly every neighborhood there is a little grocery store known as a *mekolet* ("mah-KOH-let"), which opens as early as 7 a.m. Usually family-owned, the *mekolet* sells many things, from fresh rolls to dairy products, and a nice variety of sundries. There is a warm, friendly atmosphere at the *mekolet*, and many choose to do their shopping in what is considered by some to be the neighborhood social center.

The open-air market, or *shuk*, is also a vital part of the Israeli shopping experience. Most towns have a *shuk*, where fruits and vegetables are offered at very reasonable prices. Vendors from all the stalls compete with one another, yelling prices and the advantages of their goods.

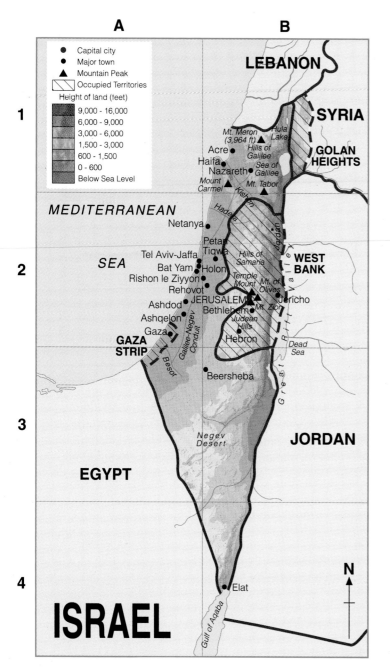

ISRAEL

Legend:
- ● Capital city
- ● Major town
- ▲ Mountain Peak
- Occupied Territories
- Height of land (feet)
  - 9,000 - 16,000
  - 6,000 - 9,000
  - 3,000 - 6,000
  - 1,500 - 3,000
  - 600 - 1,500
  - 0 - 600
  - Below Sea Level

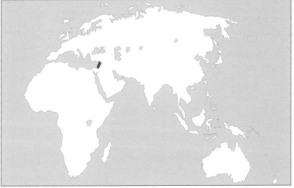

QUICK NOTES

AREA
8,020 square miles

POPULATION
5.3 million (1993 estimate)

CAPITAL
Jerusalem

MAJOR CITIES
Haifa, Tel Aviv-Jaffa

NATIONAL ANTHEM
"Hatikva" ("The Hope")

FLAG
(See page 3) "The *tallit* ("TAH-lis") in which we wrap ourselves when we pray … is our symbol. Let us take this *tallit* from its bag and unroll it before the eyes of Israel and the eyes of all nations. So I ordered a blue and white flag with the shield of David painted on it" (David Wolfsohn, 1897).
From the time this flag was presented at the First Zionist Congress, it became the flag of the Zionist movement and the Jewish community in Israel. In World War II, it was the official flag of the Jewish Brigade and, in 1948, it was adopted as Israel's national flag.

RIVERS
Jordan, Kishon, Yarkon

HIGHEST POINT
Mt. Meron (3,926 feet)

LOWEST POINT
Dead Sea (1,290 feet below sea level; the lowest point in the world)

OFFICIAL LANGUAGES
Hebrew and Arabic

MAJOR RELIGIONS
Judaism, Islam, Christianity

CURRENCY
100 agorot per shekel (US$1 = 3.04 shekels)

MAIN EXPORTS
Polished diamonds, citrus and other fruits, textiles, fertilizer and chemical products.

POLITICAL PARTIES
Labor Party, Likud Party, Sephardic Torah Guardians Association, Agudat Israel, National Religious Party

LEADERS IN POLITICS
David Ben-Gurion—first prime minister
Golda Meir—prime minister 1969–1974
Yitzak Rabin—prime minister (1992–)
Chaim Weizmann—first president
Ezer Weizmann—president (1993–)

LEADERS IN THE ARTS
Yehuda Amichai (poet)
Paul Ben-Chaim (composer)
Ofra Haza (singer)
Itzak Perlman (musician)
Amos Oz (writer)
Reuven Rubin (painter)
Yehoshua Sobol (playwright)

GLOSSARY

aliyah ("ah-lee-YUH")
"Going up." Refers to waves of Jewish immigration to Israel.

Ashkenazim ("AHSH-kuh-NAH-zim")
Jews from northern and eastern Europe.

Diaspora ("die-uh-SPORE-uh")
Dispersion of Jews after the Babylonian (587 B.C.) and Roman (A.D. 132) conquests of Palestine.

falafel ("fuh-LAH-fehl")
Ground chickpeas mixed with spices, garlic, and onion, then shaped into balls and fried.

Histadrut ("hiss-tahd-root")
General Federation of Labor, the most important workers' union in Israel.

Holocaust
Killing of six million European Jews by the Nazis during World War II.

Intifada ("IN-tuh-FAH-duh")
Civil disobedience and unrest begun in 1987 by Palestinian Arabs to protest Israeli occupation of the West Bank and Gaza Strip.

kibbutz ("key-BOOTZ")
Israeli collective farm where people work and live together, sharing all their possessions.

kibbutznik ("key-BOOTZ-nik")
Residents of the kibbutz.

Knesset ("kuh-NESS-et")
The parliament, or governing body, of Israel.

kosher ("KOE-sher")
Food that has been prepared according to Jewish dietary laws.

menorah ("muh-noh-ruh")
Seven-branched candelabrum of traditional Jewish worship and the official Israeli emblem.

Palestine
Historically, the area between the Jordan River and the Mediterranean Sea in which most of the biblical narrative is located.

rabbi
Spiritual leader of a Jewish congregation.

Sabbath
The seventh day of the week (Saturday), set aside by the Fourth Commandment for rest and worship and observed as such by Jews.

sabra
Nickname for Israelis, derived from name of a cactus fruit grown in Israel that is tough on the outside but sweet inside.

Sephardim ("suh-FAR-dim")
Jews from Aegean, Mediterranean, Balkan, and Middle Eastern countries.

shofar ("show-fahr")
Ram's horn, used in ancient times in religious ceremonies as a signal in battle, and still in use today.

ulpan ("ool-PAHN")
An institute specially designed to teach Jewish immigrants about the cultures of Israel, and to offer Hebrew language lessons.

Zionism
The effort of the Jews to regain and retain their biblical homeland, based on God's promise in the Bible that Israel would belong to the Jews.

BIBLIOGRAPHY

Abba Eban: *Personal Witness—Israel Through My Eyes*, G.P. Putnam's Sons, New York, 1992.

Feinstein, Steve. *Israel in Pictures*. Minneapolis: Lerner Publications, 1989.

Grossman, David. *Sleeping on a Wire: Conversations with Palestinians in Israel*. New York: Farrar, Straus and Giroux, 1993.

Harper, Paul. *The Arab-Israeli Conflict*. New York: Bookwright Press, 1990.

Metz, Helen Chapin (editor). *Israel, a Country Study*. Washington, D.C.: U.S. Government Printing Office, 1990.

Reich, Bernard and Gershon Kieval. *Israel, Land of Tradition and Conflict*. Boulder: Westview Press, 1993.

Rabinovich, Abraham. *Israel*. London: Flint River Press Ltd, 1989.

Winter, Dick. *Culture Shock! Israel*. Portland: Graphic Arts, 1992.

Wright, Martin and Paul Cossali. Israel and the Palestinians. Harlow: Longman, 1989.

INDEX

INDEX

INDEX

PICTURE CREDITS
Werner Braun: 1, 4, 6, 9, 15, 29,
    30, 35, 39, 43, 67, 83, 86, 95, 98,
    101, 106, 110, 119
The Image Bank: 3, 14, 16, 41, 47,
    49, 59, 63, 64, 68, 74, 79, 84
Israeli Embassy: 11, 26, 27, 28, 31,
    33
Life File Photo Library: 7, 18, 32,
    34, 36, 37, 38, 44, 46, 48, 51, 53,
    66, 78, 80, 85, 88, 89, 97, 113,
    116, 117, 118
Anat Rotem-Braun: 5, 10, 40, 45,
    54, 60, 61, 62, 70, 71, 72, 90, 92,
    94, 96, 99, 103, 104, 108, 109,
    112, 115, 120
Jamie Simson: 13, 17, 19, 20, 21,
    23, 25, 50, 52, 55, 56, 57, 58, 75,
    77, 91, 100, 123